Excel Pivot Tables & Charts
A Step By Step Visual Guide

Excel 2016/2013
Practice Projects & Solutions Included for Beginners

By
A. J. Wright

Excel Pivot Tables & Charts
A Step By Step Visual Guide
Copyright © 2019 A. J. Wright

All rights reserved. No part of this book may be reproduced, stored in a retrieval system, or transmitted in any form or by any means, without the prior written permission of the publisher, except in the case of brief quotations embedded in critical articles or reviews. Every effort has been made in the preparation of this book to ensure the accuracy of the information presented. However, the information contained in this book is sold without warranty, either express or implied. The author/publisher, its dealers and distributors will not be held liable for any damages caused or alleged to be caused directly or indirectly by this book. The author/publisher has endeavored to provide trademark information about all of the companies and products mentioned in this book. However, he cannot guarantee the accuracy of this information.

Trademarks: Microsoft®, Excel® and Word® are registered trademarks or trademarks of Microsoft Corporation in the United States and/or other countries.

First published: **February 2018**
Second Edition: **June 2019**

Table of Contents

How to Use This Book	5
Download Link for Exercise Files	5
1. Introduction to Pivot Tables	6
What is A Pivot Table?	6
Basic Concepts	9
Conditions to Create a Pivot Table	10
Limitations of a Pivot Table	10
2. Creating A Pivot Table	12
Source of Data	12
Structure of the Pivot Table	13
Creating Your First Pivot Table	13
3. Creating A Pivot Chart	22
How to Drill-Down Pivot Table Data	29
Adding More Rows (categories) to Pivot Table	30
How to Create A Pivot Table Chart	31
4. Slicers & Advanced Filtering	37
Practice Project 1	37
Timeline Slicer	38
Slicer	45
Additional Information	47
Advanced Filtering	50
5. Calculations in Pivot Tables	55
Calculated Fields	55
Practice Project 2	55
Adding A Basic Calculated Field	56
Removing Or Changing Calculated Fields	64
Inserting Logic Fields (if...then)	65
6. Customizing Pivot Tables	67
Making Major Cosmetic Changes	68
Making Minor Cosmetic Changes	69

7. Using VBA Macro Language to Create Pivot Tables	72
Introduction to VBA	72
Why Use Macros with Your Pivot Table Reports?	72
Recording Your First Macro	73
Using VBA to Create Pivot Tables	77
Visual Basic Editor	78
Visual Basic Tools	79
Understanding Object-Oriented Code	80
Writing Code to Handle Any Size Data Range	80
Using Super-Variables: Object Variables	81
Using With and End With to Shorten Code	82
Building a Pivot Table in Excel VBA	83
Practice Project 3	83
Adding Fields to the Data Area	85
8: Advanced Tips, Tricks & Techniques	90

How to Use This Book

This book can be used as a tutorial or quick reference visual guide. It is intended for users who are comfortable with the basics of Microsoft® Excel® and are now ready to build upon this skill by learning *Pivot Tables and Charts*.

This book assumes you already know how to create, open, save, and modify an Excel® workbook and have a general familiarity with the Excel® toolbar (Ribbon).

Most of the examples in this book use **Microsoft Excel 2016**. However, the functionality and formulas can be applied with **Microsoft Excel version 2013**. Although the screenshots in this book use Microsoft Excel 2016, functionality and display are not very much different if you are using Excel 2013.

Please always back-up your work and save often as we go. A good best practice when attempting any new functionality is to create a copy of the original spreadsheet and implement your changes on the copied spreadsheet. Should anything go wrong, you then have the original spreadsheet to fall back on.

Download Link for Exercise Files
The exercise files we will use later in this book are available for download at the following website: **https://goo.gl/e1SsZV**.

Chapter 1: Introduction to Pivot Tables

Databases contain raw data on various topics, and are usually arranged in a tabular form. In many cases, data overload may make it difficult to use the information and convert it into relevant knowledge.

What is A Pivot Table?

A pivot table is a simple, yet powerful, technique which enables Excel users to turn the data overload into well-organized and meaningful knowledge.

By using a pivot table, users can perform various calculations on their data, such as calculating the average, counting, finding the minimum and the maximum values and so on.

Furthermore, the pivot table enables us to filter and sort the data easily and quickly. Users may focus on some or all parts of the data, even when the data tables are huge (some databases may contain a million or more records); thus users can obtain their desired data clearly and concisely.

A single data table can be used to create dozens of reports and charts for analyzing the data, with many cross-sections, simply by dragging fields to the appropriate locations.

Thus, the pivot table enables us to better understand processes and trends. It is also a useful tool for decision making. The pivot table data can be based on an existing Excel file or on other databases (i.e. Access or an SQL-based database).

Since a picture is worth a thousand words, here are some examples of pivot tables, derived from the same database of Fig. 1.0 showing the details of factory employees:

Employee No.	Start Date	Section	Department	Role	Gender	City	Monthly Salary
W1331	02/01/2006	Sales and Marketing	Marketing	Person Marketing	Female	Detroit	2,875
W1332	09/09/2005	Sales and Marketing	Marketing	Person Marketing	Female	Detroit	3,031
W1333	09/02/2009	Sales and Marketing	Marketing	Person Marketing	Female	Los Angeles	3,035
W1334	06/07/2007	Sales and Marketing	Marketing	Person Marketing	Female	Detroit	3,293
W1335	12/11/2009	Sales and Marketing	Marketing	Person Marketing	Female	Detroit	3,253
W1336	06/05/2005	Sales and Marketing	Marketing	Person Marketing	Female	Los Angeles	3,136
W1337	02/05/2002	Sales and Marketing	Marketing	Person Marketing	Female	Detroit	3,346
W1338	01/03/2003	Sales and Marketing	Marketing	Person Marketing	Male	Miami	2,864
W1339	03/10/2006	Sales and Marketing	Marketing	Person Marketing	Male	San Diego	3,178
W1340	04/11/2005	Sales and Marketing	Marketing	Person Marketing	Female	Detroit	3,007
W1341	11/05/2006	Sales and Marketing	Marketing	Person Marketing	Female	Los Angeles	3,027
W1112	02/12/2003	Sales and Marketing	Sales	salesperson	Male	New Jersey	3,741
W1113	04/09/2011	Sales and Marketing	Sales	salesperson	Male	Miami	4,015
W1114	06/08/2010	Sales and Marketing	Sales	salesperson	Female	Los Angeles	4,189
W1115	05/07/2008	Sales and Marketing	Sales	salesperson	Male	San Diego	3,651
W1116	04/06/2009	Sales and Marketing	Sales	salesperson	Male	Detroit	3,906
W1117	03/08/2004	Sales and Marketing	Sales	salesperson	Male	New Jersey	3,785
W1118	08/06/2011	Sales and Marketing	Sales	salesperson	Female	Detroit	3,707
W1119	02/05/2004	Sales and Marketing	Sales	salesperson	Female	New Jersey	3,916
W1120	07/12/2007	Sales and Marketing	Sales	salesperson	Female	Los Angeles	4,085
W1121	03/12/2010	Sales and Marketing	Sales	salesperson	Male	New Jersey	4,250
W1122	10/10/2001	Sales and Marketing	Sales	salesperson	Male	San Diego	4,241
W1123	02/01/2011	Sales and Marketing	Sales	salesperson	Male	Miami	3,666
W1124	04/01/2003	Sales and Marketing	Sales	salesperson	Female	Detroit	4,397
W1125	01/05/2011	Sales and Marketing	Sales	salesperson	Male	Los Angeles	3,662
W1126	08/11/2008	Sales and Marketing	Sales	salesperson	Female	Detroit	4,349
W1127	06/04/2008	Sales and Marketing	Sales	salesperson	Male	Miami	3,973
W1128	02/10/2006	Sales and Marketing	Sales	salesperson	Female	Los Angeles	3,661
W1129	12/04/2011	Sales and Marketing	Sales	salesperson	Female	Los Angeles	3,682
W1130	01/12/2002	Sales and Marketing	Sales	salesperson	Female	New Jersey	4,276

Fig. 1.0: Database of factory employees

The following pivot tables were derived from the database above: Number of employees in each department:

Department	Count of Employee No.
Accounting	3
accounting department	6
Engraving	453
headquarters	3
Human Resources	9
Marketing	12
Sales	204
Welding	310
Grand Total	**1000**

Fig. 1.1: Number of employees in each department

Distribution of genders in each department:

Count of Employee No.	Gender	
Department	Female	Male
Accounting	2	1
accounting department	4	2
Engraving	226	227
headquarters	2	1
Human Resources	4	5
Marketing	9	3
Sales	106	98
Welding	144	166

Fig. 1.2: Distribution of genders in each department

Average salary in each department:

Average of Monthly Salary	
Department	Total
Accounting	4,551.00
Accounting department	2,947.67
Engraving	2,027.04
Headquarters	4,730.33
Human Resources	3,037.22
Marketing	3,195.75
Sales	3,999.12
Welding	2,127.72
Grand Total	2,504.88

Fig. 1.3: Average salary in each department

Average salary in each section, by role:

Average of Monthly Salary	Section		
Role	Management	Manufacturing	Sales and Marketing
Accountant	4,551		
Bookkeeper	2,773		
Department Manager	5,140	4,602	4,449
Engineer		7,474	
Manager	3,864	3,920	4,206
Person Marketing			3,095
Practical Engineer		7,385	
Production Worker		1,827	
Recruitment Coordinator	1,843		
salesperson			3,999
Senior Recruitment Coordinator	4,737		
Grand Total	3,359	2,071	3,957

Fig. 1.4: Average salary in each section by role

Basic Concepts

This chapter presents basic concepts relating to pivot tables. While studying and practicing, the following concepts will become clearer:

Data Table: A raw data set, arranged in a table. This can be used as the source of a pivot table.

Pivot Table: A table that displays data in different intersections, as described in this book.

Column: A vertical section of the table consisting of data of the same type, i.e. first name, ID, city etc.

Field: The column's header is called a "field".

Cell: The cell is the intersection of a row and a column, and contains the data of the table.

Item: The data in a cell. For example, New York and Detroit are items in the "City" field.

Record: A data collection which appears in one row and belongs to the same entity, e.g. all the table data which displays information regarding one person.

Conditions to Create a Pivot Table

Necessary Conditions:
- Each column must have a title.
- The title should be written in a single row.
- In a column, all the items should be of the same data type (numbers, dates or strings).
- The data table should not contain any merged cells.
- The data table should not contain subtotals or grand totals.
- Empty rows or columns should not remain within the table (if an empty row or column remains, Excel will treat the table as two different ones).
- After creating a pivot table, do not change the titles of the fields, otherwise the pivot table values will be deleted.

Desirable Conditions
- Unique names for each column (when two fields are given the same name, the title of the second field will be appended at end with 2, e.g. "salary2").
- Complete data for all records (when data is missing, the calculations will only be applied to the available records. This can be observed in the cases of calculations such as averages, etc).

Limitations of a Pivot Table
- Number of pivot table reports in the worksheet: Limited by the available memory.
- Unique items for each field.
- Row fields or column fields in the pivot table report: Limited by the available memory.
- Report filter in the pivot table report: 256 (May be limited by the available memory).
- Value fields in the pivot table report: 256.
- Formulas for calculated items in the pivot table report: Limited by the available memory.

Important Note: Due to the limitations of the pivot table, and depending on your personal computer data, you may prefer to save the exercises appearing in this book in a separate file or worksheet for each chapter.

Chapter 2: Creating A Pivot Table

Creating pivot tables in your Microsoft Excel 2013/2016 is a fast procedure, consisting of 3 **basic steps**:

Step 1. Selecting the data source and table location.
Step 2. Dragging in the desirable fields.
Step 3. Using the tools in the ribbon for calculations and formatting (most of them can be operated by right-clicking the corresponding area in the pivot table).

Source of Data
The data source for the pivot table can be:
- The current Excel file
- Another Excel file
- Other file types, such as:
    1. Access
    2. SQL database

Selecting from a data table in the current file:
- Once you have pressed INSERT PivotTable, the entire table will be selected automatically.
- The range can be modified by dragging and selecting another range.

Selecting from a data table in another Excel file:
- Before creating a pivot table, make sure that the file that contains the data table is open.
- Using the Windows task bar, select the data file.
- Select the desired range.

We will discuss about how to create pivot tables from other data types later in this book. You should follow along the steps in this example. So use the link below to download the sample spreadsheet:

https://goo.gl/9mLYRv

Structure of the Pivot Table

As you may have noticed in the above example, the Pivot table screen is divided into 3 main areas:

1. The list of fields
2. The pivot table areas
3. The pivot table

List of fields
The list of fields contains the column titles of the selected range.

Areas
The pivot table is divided into four areas that the desired fields can be dragged into:

- **Columns** - where fields to be shown in columns are dragged.
- **Rows** - where fields to be shown in rows are dragged.
- **Values** - where fields on which calculations are to be performed (average, minimum, maximum, count, standard deviation, etc.) are dragged.
- **Filters** – where fields to be used as a filter are dragged.

The COLUMNS and ROWS form the pivots of the pivot table.

Creating Your First Pivot Table
Step 1. Double-click on the sample spreadsheet you just downloaded to open it inside your Microsoft Excel application. The sheet contains the data of the pivot table we want to create. It will open inside Sheet1 and will look like Fig. 2.0 below:

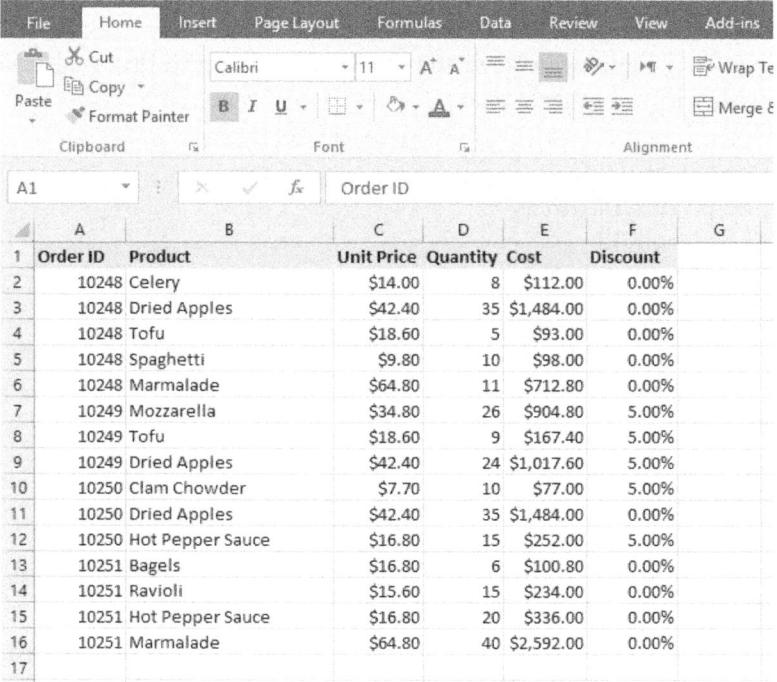

Fig. 2.0: Sample Spreadsheet data loaded on sheet 1

Step 2. Select Sheet2 by clicking on it at the bottom of the window. Select the cell where the pivot table will be created in. In our example, it is the **A1** cell on **Sheet2**. The following window will appear:

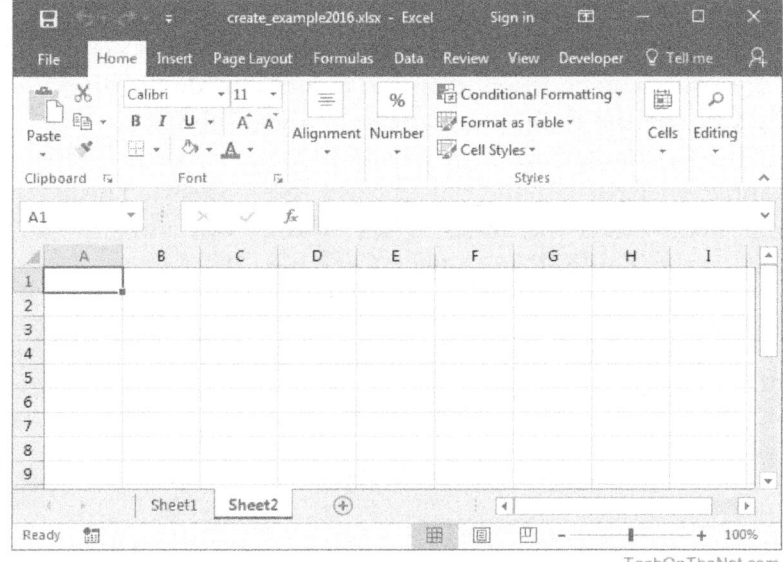

Fig. 2.1: Sheet2 showing Cell A1 for new pivot table

Step 3. In the **INSERT** tab. Then lick the button **PivotTable**:

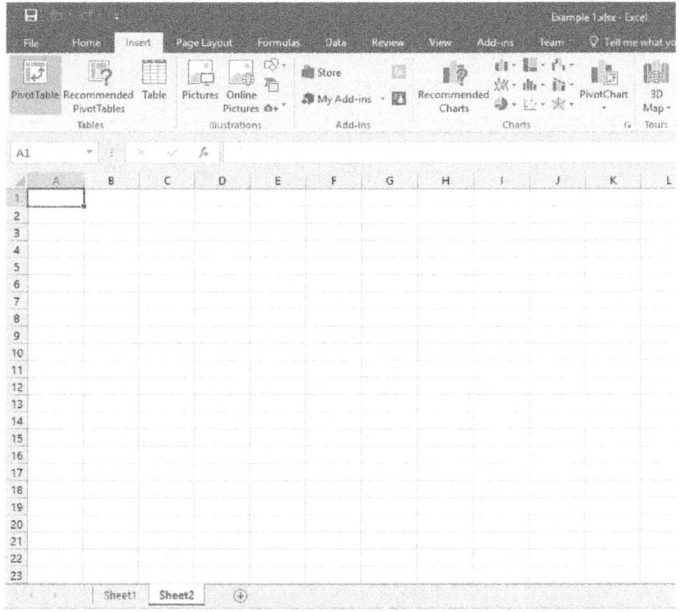

Fig. 2.2: Selecting *PivotTable* from the *Insert* Tool Bar

A new window - **Create PivotTable** - will appear as shown in Fig. 2.3. Ensure you choose the option **Select a table or range** under the **Choose the data you want to analyze** sub-heading. Note that in Sheet1, our data has 16 rows and F columns. Therefore in this sample, we have selected cells A1 to F16 on Sheet1. This is indicated by the code **Sheet1!$A$1:$F$16**. Copy and paste this code in the **Table/Range** field. Click the OK button.

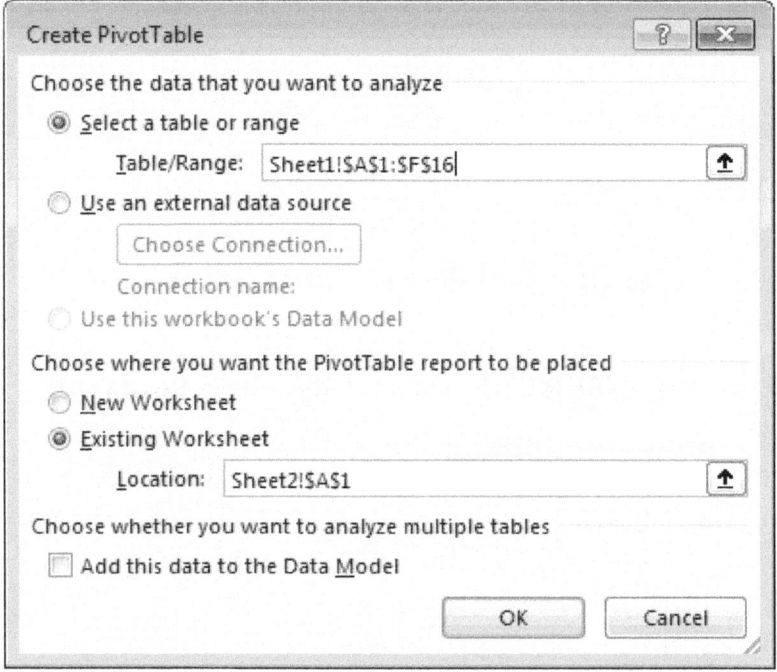

Fig. 2.3: The completed *Create PivotTable* window

Important Note: The pivot table can be placed in the same worksheet as the data table, or in another worksheet as we have just done. Please note that if you choose to place the pivot table *on the same sheet* as the data table, **you will not be able to delete an entire row**. This is true for both Excel versions 2016 and 2013.

The pivot table (compressed a little to save space) should now look simlar to that shown in Fig. 2.4:

Excel Pivot Tables & Charts

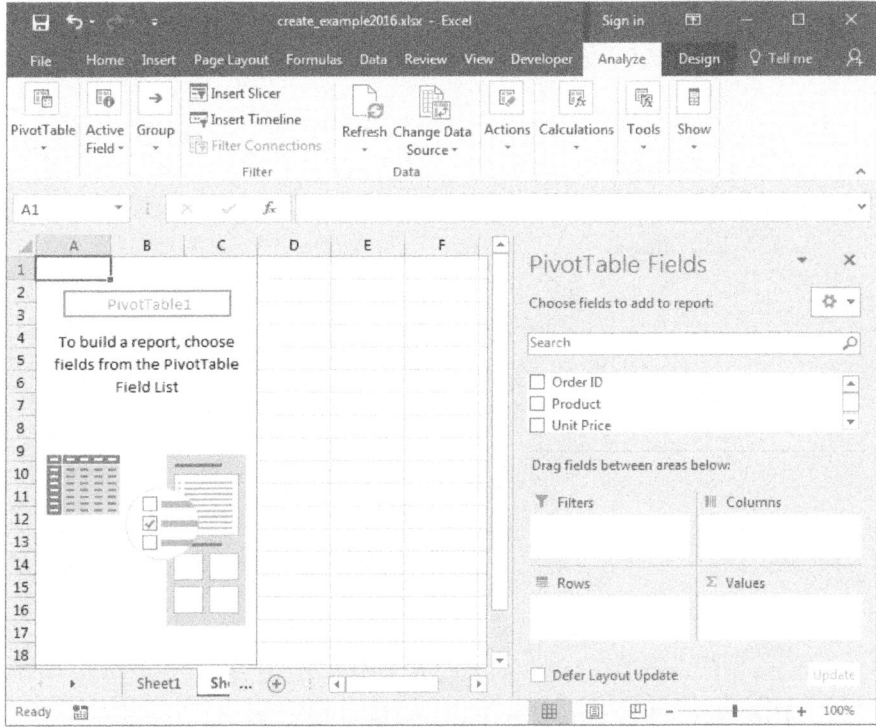

Fig. 2.4: New Pivot table opened

Now we select the fields to be added to our report. The screenshot in Fig. 2.5 shows 2 checkboxes beside **Order ID** and **Quantity** fields selected.

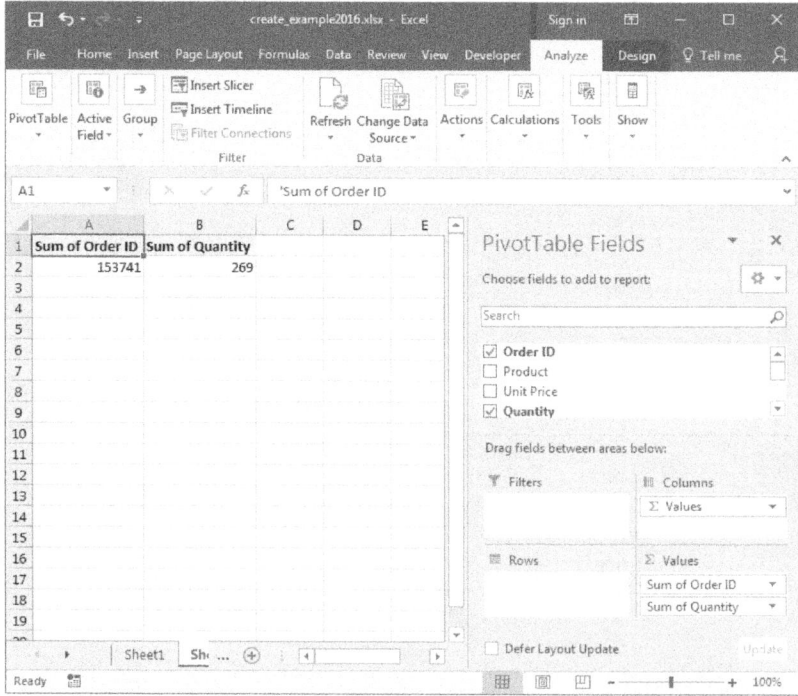

Fig. 2.5: Choosing the fields to be added to our report

Now, in the section marked **Values** on the bottom right, we click on and drag the **Sum of Order ID** to the empty box in the **Rows** section (indicated by the red arrow in Fig. 2.6).

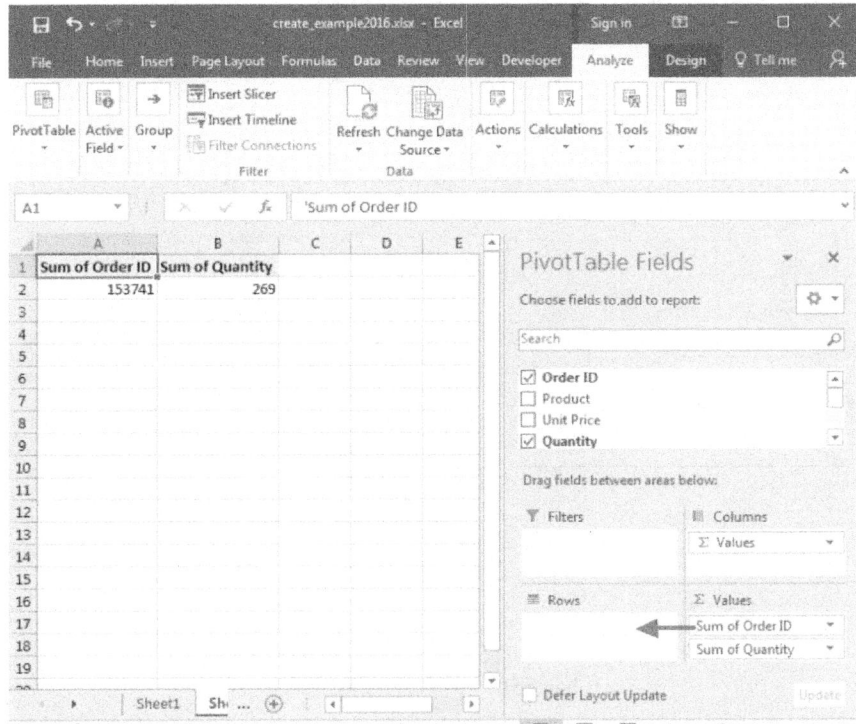

Fig. 2.6: Dragging the *Sum of Order ID* to the empty box in the *Rows* section

Fig. 2.7 below shows the updated report:

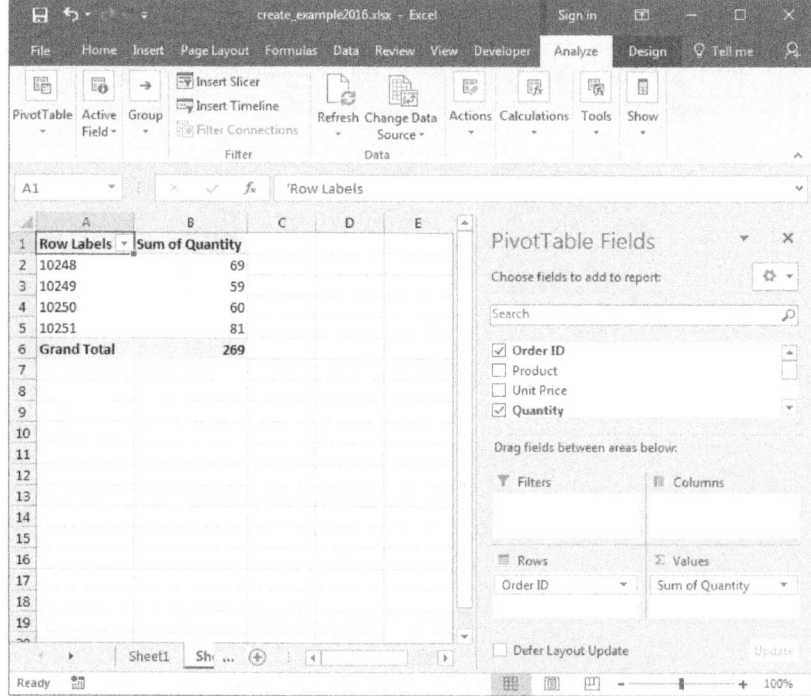

Fig. 2.7: Updated report

Now, we prefer to have the cell A1 show **Order ID**, not **Row Labels** as it is currently. To change it, we just select the cell A1 and type in **Order ID**.

It is preferable to give the fields short names, since they will appear as titles in the pivot table. Avoid using the words "**sum**", "**average**", "**minimum**", or "**maximu**m" in the titles, since they are added automatically when calculations are performed. This will prevent poor titles like "**Sum of Sum of Salaries**" from appearing.

Finally, we can now see in the screenshot of Fig. 2.8 that the pivot table (the report) is completed because the total quantity for each Order ID is now displayed:

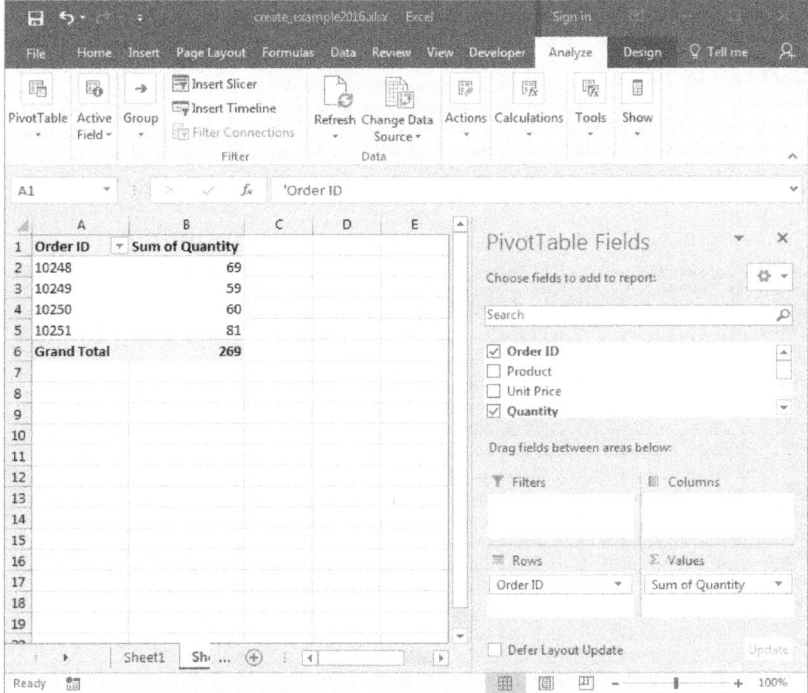

Fig. 2.8: Completed Pivot Table

Chapter 3: Creating A Pivot Chart

We will use the spreadsheet named "**FruitSales.xlsx**" in the exercise folder that you downloaded under the section "How to Use This Book" to create another Pivot Table, and then a Pivot Table Chart, step by step.

Fig 3.0 shows a portion of this spreadsheet (truncated due to space limitation).

	A	B	C	D	E	F	G	H	I
1	REGION	SALES PERSON FIRST NAME	SALES PERSON LAST NAME	SALES PERSON ID	QUARTER	APPLES	ORANGES	MANGOS	TOTAL
2	Central	Bob	Taylor	1174	1	1,810	2,039	1,771	5,620
3	Central	Helen	Smith	833	1	102	354	59	516
4	Central	Jill	Johnson	200	1	93	322	54	469
5	Central	Sally	Morton	500	1	595	824	556	1,975
6	Central	Sam	Becker	800	1	863	1,092	824	2,779
7	East	Abbey	Williams	690	1	346	237	260	843
8	East	John	Dower	255	1	260	178	195	633
9	East	John	Wilson	300	1	286	196	215	696
10	East	Mary	Nelson	600	1	315	215	236	766
11	East	Sarah	Taylor	900	1	381	261	285	927
12	West	Alex	Steller	1000	1	163	212	127	502
13	West	Billy	Winchester	1156	1	179	234	140	552
14	West	Helen	Simpson	817	1	148	193	116	457
15	West	Jack	Smith	100	1	111	145	87	343
16	West	Joe	Tanner	400	1	122	160	96	377
17	West	Peter	Graham	700	1	134	175	105	415
18	Central	Bob	Taylor	1174	2	113	390	65	567
19	Central	Helen	Smith	833	2	1,006	1,393	940	3,338
20	Central	Jill	Johnson	200	2	774	1,071	723	2,568
21	Central	Sally	Morton	500	2	1,295	1,638	1,236	4,169
22	Central	Sam	Becker	800	2	2,806	3,160	2,745	8,711
23	East	Abbey	Williams	690	2	1,674	1,494	1,531	4,699
24	East	John	Dower	255	2	762	680	697	2,139
25	East	John	Wilson	300	2	991	884	906	2,781

Fig. 3.0: FruitSales.xlsx spreadsheet

First we will determine the **'total sales by region'** and then we will build upon this by adding the **'quarterly sales by region'**:

1. Open the **FruitSales.xlsx** spreadsheet and highlight **cells A1:I65**
2. From the Ribbon select **INSERT** : **PivotTable**.

The dialogue box in Fig. 3.1 should appear:

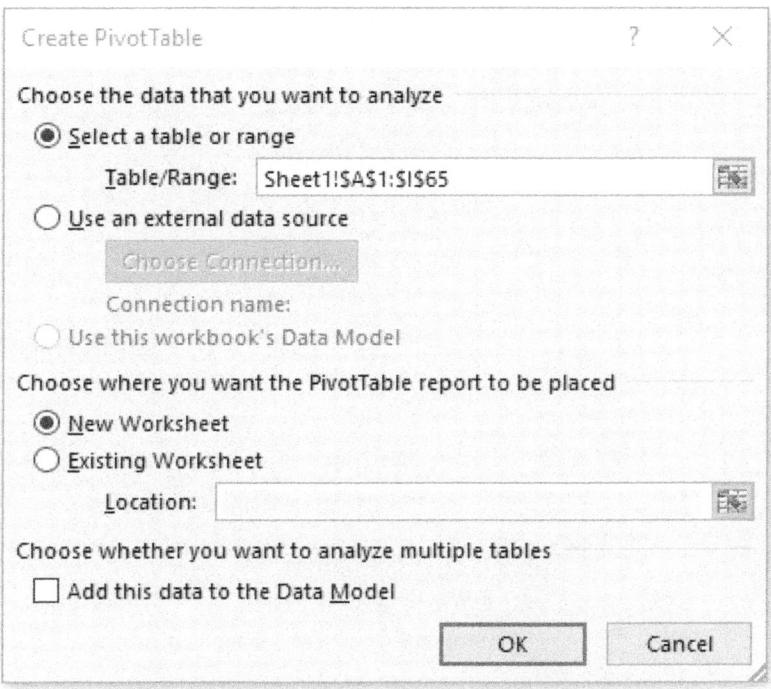

Fig. 3.1: Create PivotTable dialogue box

3. Ensure that the **New Worksheet** radio button is selected
4. Click the **OK** button

A new tab will be created in Sheet2 and appear similar to the Fig 3.2:

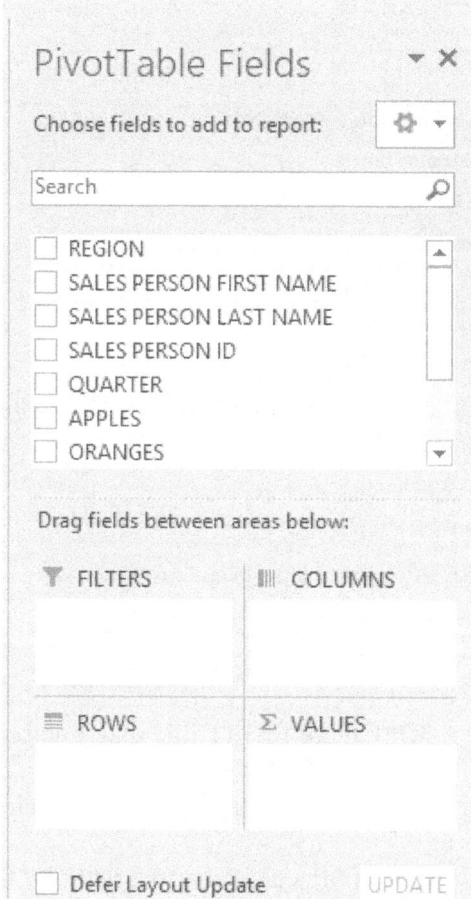

Fig. 3.2: PivotTable Fields created

Next, we'll "categorize" our report and select a calculation value.

5. Inside the PivotTable Fields pane click the **REGION** box or drag this field to **Rows** section.
6. Inside the PivotTable Fields pane click the **TOTAL** box (you may need to first scroll down a little to reach this box) or drag this field to the **Values** section.

Please see Fig. 3.3 for an illustration of steps 5 & 6.

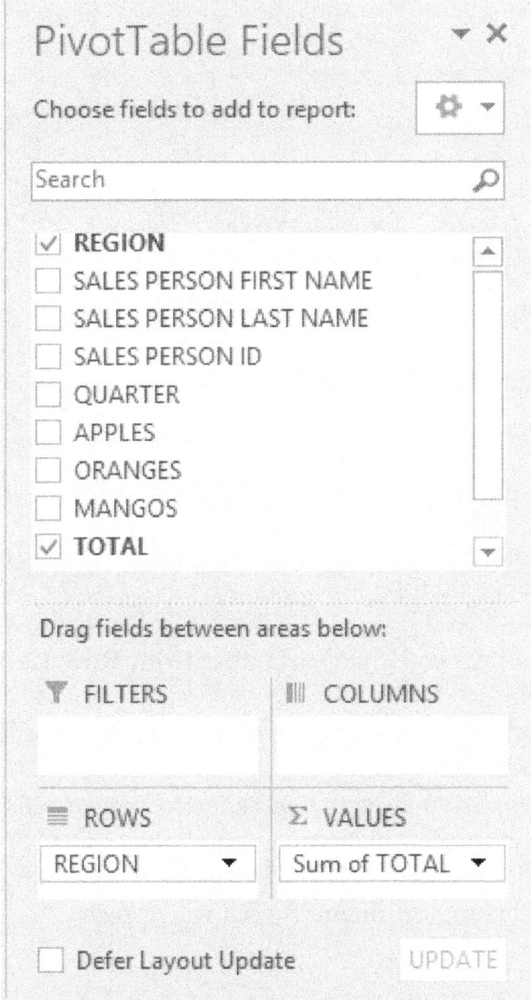

Fig. 3.3: PivotTable Fields with REGION and TOTAL selected

The following Fig 3.4 should be displayed on the left side of your screen. Note that the format is not very easy to read.

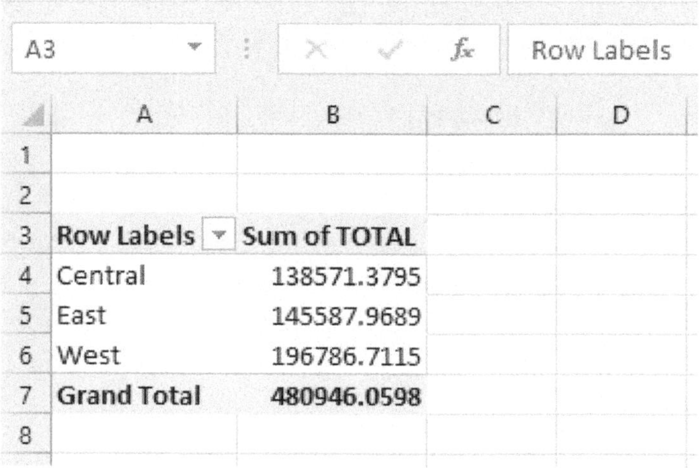

	A	B	C	D
1				
2				
3	Row Labels	Sum of TOTAL		
4	Central	138571.3795		
5	East	145587.9689		
6	West	196786.7115		
7	Grand Total	480946.0598		
8				

Fig. 3.4: Unformatted PivotTable

7. We can change the column labels and format of the numbers. In the below example:

a. Select cell **A3** and change the text from **Row Labels** to **REGION**.
b. Select cell **B3** and change the text from **Sum of TOTAL** to **TOTAL SALES**
c. You may also change the currency format in cells **B4 to B7**. In the below example, the format was changed to U.S. dollars with zero decimal places. You can do this by highlighting all the 4 cells and right clicking on them. Fig 3.5 will appear:

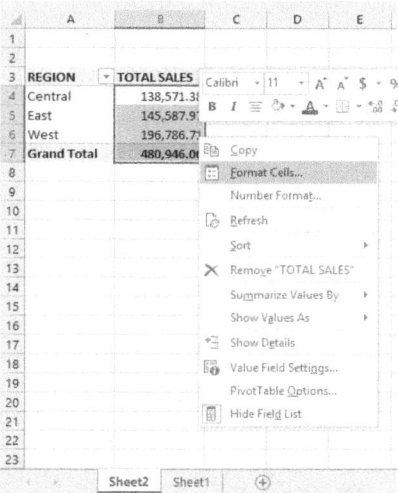

Fig. 3.5: Changing the currency format

When the **Format Cells** window appears as in Fig. 3.6, click on Currency.

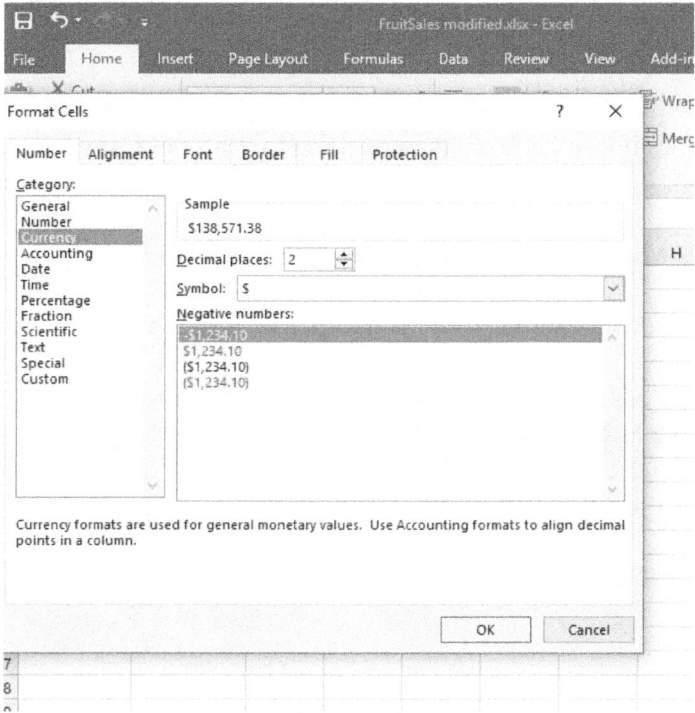

Fig. 3.6: Selecting $ currency

Make sure "$" is selected in the **Symbol** field. Then click **OK**.

Fig. 3.7 shows the formatted report.

	A	B
3	REGION	TOTAL SALES
4	Central	$138,571.38
5	East	$145,587.97
6	West	$196,786.71
7	Grand Total	$480,946.06

Fig. 3.7: Formatted report

To enhance the report we're going to add **Quarter** columns. This "level" dimension will provide greater detail of the total fruit sales.

8. Inside the PivotTable Fields pane **drag** the **QUARTER** field to the **Columns** section.

Important Note: Excel is reading the Quarter value as numeric, therefore if you click, instead of dragging the field to the **Columns** section, Excel will apply a calculation. If this happens click the drop-down-box of **Sum of QUARTER** in the **Values** section and select the option **Move to Column Labels**.

We now have **QUARTER** added to the summary.

9. Select cell **B3** and change the text from **Column Labels** to **BY QUARTER**.
10. Then change the labels for cells **B4, C4, D4**, and **E4** by adding the abbreviation text **QTR** in front of each quarter number.

Fig. 3.8 shows the formatted report:

	A	B	C	D	E	F
1						
2						
3	TOTAL SALES	BY QUARTER				
4	REGION	QTR 1	QTR 2	QTR 3	QTR 4	Grand Total
5	Central	$11,358.90	$19,352.24	$34,097.24	$73,763.00	$138,571.38
6	East	$3,864.53	$19,343.19	$38,810.81	$83,569.44	$145,587.97
7	West	$2,646.45	$23,585.90	$42,590.48	$127,963.88	$196,786.71
8	Grand Total	$17,869.88	$62,281.33	$115,498.53	$285,296.31	$480,946.06
9						

Fig. 3.8: Formatted report with *QUARTER* added to the summary

How to Drill-Down Pivot Table Data

Before we continue with our Pivot Table report examples, let's say you wanted to investigate further why the Central region's Q1 results are so much higher than the other two regions.

Pivot Tables allow you to **double-click on any calculated value to see the detail of that cell.** You may also **right-click** on the calculated value and select **Show Details**. This will create a new worksheet containing a table with the details of the calculated value. Please see Fig. 3.9 below.

1. **Right-click** on cell **B5** and select **Show Details**.

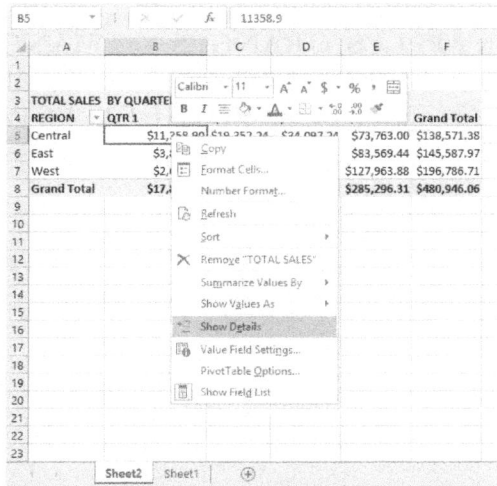

Fig. 3.9: Right-clicking to investigate the Central region's Q1 results

A new worksheet containing a table with the details of the calculated value in cell **B5** is shown in Fig. 3.10:

	A	B	C	D	E	F	G	H	I
1	REGION	SALES PERSON FIRST NAME	SALES PERSON LAST NAME	SALES PERSON ID	QUARTER	APPLES	ORANGES	MANGOS	TOTAL
2	Central	Bob	Taylor	1174	1	1810	2039	1771	5620
3	Central	Helen	Smith	833	1	102.3	354.2	59.4	515.9
4	Central	Jill	Johnson	200	1	93	322	54	469
5	Central	Sally	Morton	500	1	595	824	556	1975
6	Central	Sam	Becker	800	1	863	1092	824	2779

Fig. 3.10: details of calculated value in cell **B5**

As can be seen from Fig. 3.10, **Bob Taylor** made the highest sale and is the reason why the Central region's Q1 results are so much higher than the other two regions.

2. To delete the table, right-click on **Sheet3** and select **Delete**.

Adding More Rows (categories) to Pivot Table

From our original Pivot Table report, we'll extend our analysis by adding the individual fruit sales to our summary.

1. Drag the **QUARTER** field from the **COLUMNS** section to the **ROWS** section.

2. Drag the fields **APPLES**, **ORANGES**, and **MANGOS** to the **VALUES** section of the **PivotTable Fields** pane, making sure you place the fruit fields <u>on top of</u> the **TOTAL SALES** value.

The report should look like Fig. 3.11 below:

REGION	Sum of APPLES	Sum of ORANGES	Sum of MANGOS	TOTAL SALES
⊟ Central	$43,480.80	$53,278.36	$41,812.22	$138,571.38
QTR 1	$3,463.30	$4,631.20	$3,264.40	$11,358.90
QTR 2	$5,991.58	$7,651.83	$5,708.83	$19,352.24
QTR 3	$10,633.90	$13,280.11	$10,183.23	$34,097.24
QTR 4	$23,392.02	$27,715.22	$22,655.76	$73,763.00
⊟ East	$50,625.74	$47,117.45	$47,844.78	$145,587.97
QTR 1	$1,587.33	$1,086.71	$1,190.49	$3,864.53
QTR 2	$6,890.84	$6,149.31	$6,303.04	$19,343.19
QTR 3	$13,583.13	$12,501.75	$12,725.94	$38,810.81
QTR 4	$28,564.45	$27,379.68	$27,625.30	$83,569.44
⊟ West	$69,750.20	$65,258.99	$61,777.51	$196,786.71
QTR 1	$856.43	$1,118.76	$671.26	$2,646.45
QTR 2	$7,819.45	$8,253.15	$7,513.30	$23,585.90
QTR 3	$15,334.91	$14,073.84	$13,181.73	$42,590.48
QTR 4	$45,739.42	$41,813.23	$40,411.22	$127,963.88
Grand Total	$163,856.75	$165,654.80	$151,434.51	$480,946.06

Fig. 3.11: Additional rows added to PivotTable

How to Create A Pivot Table Chart

In this section, you will learn how to create and format a Pivot Table chart. Follow these steps:

1. From the **PivotTable Fields** pane <u>uncheck</u> the **TOTAL** field (Fig. 3.12 shows TOTAL SALES field unselected).

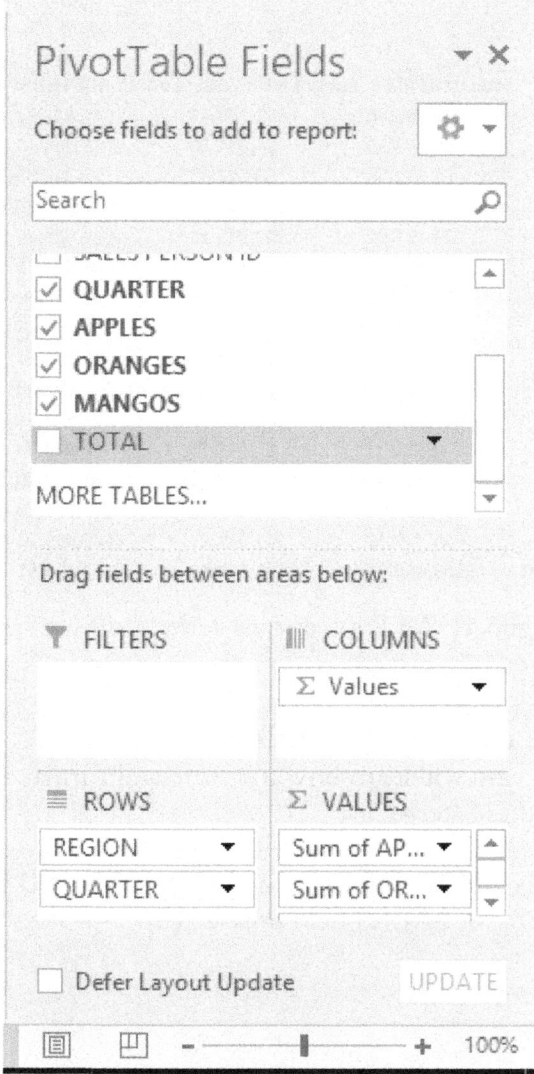

Fig. 3.12: TOTAL field unchecked

2. From the **PivotTable Tools** Ribbon select the tab **Analyze: PivotChart** (Fig. 3.13).

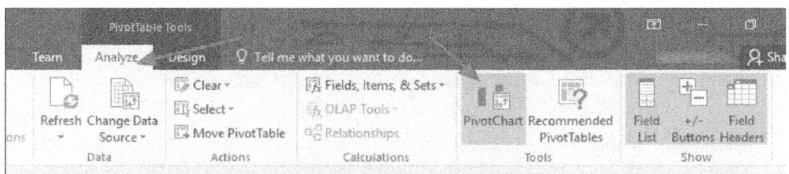

Fig. 3.13: Selecting PivotChart tool

Important Note: If you do not see the **PivotTable Tools** option on your Ribbon, **click any PivotTable cell**. This toolbar option only appears when a PivotTable field is active.

The dialogue in Fig. 3.14 box should appear:

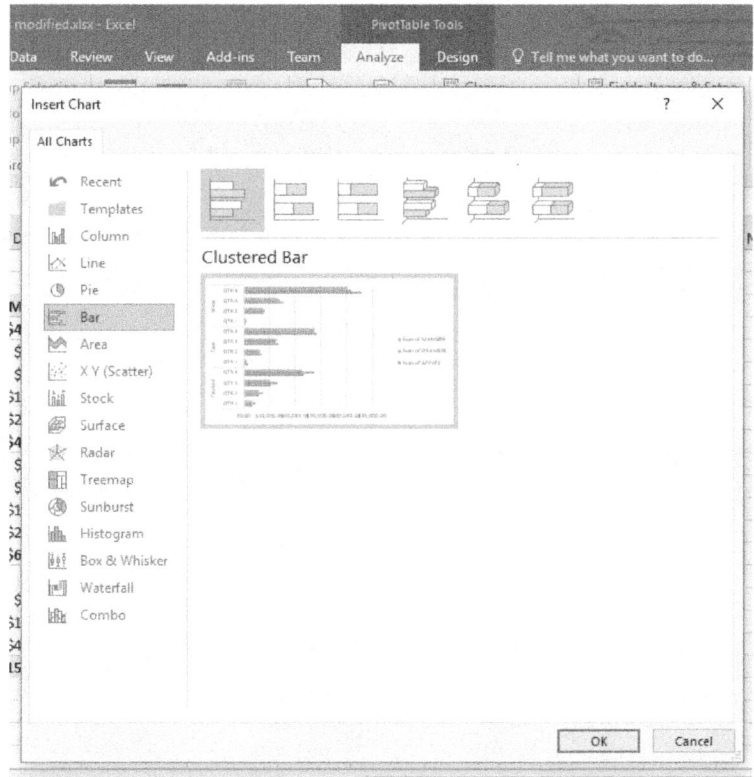

Fig. 3.14: Selecting Bar chart from PivotTable Chart

3. Select the **Bar** option.
4. Click the **OK** button.

The chart shown in Fig. 3.15 should now be displayed:

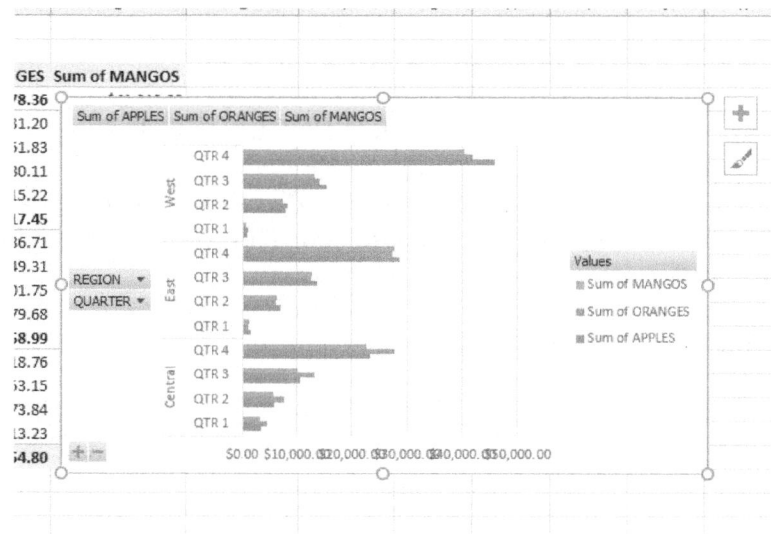

Fig. 3.15: New Bar Chart is displayed

5. Drag the chart below the Pivot Table report summary and expand the width to allow for easier viewing (Fig. 3.16):

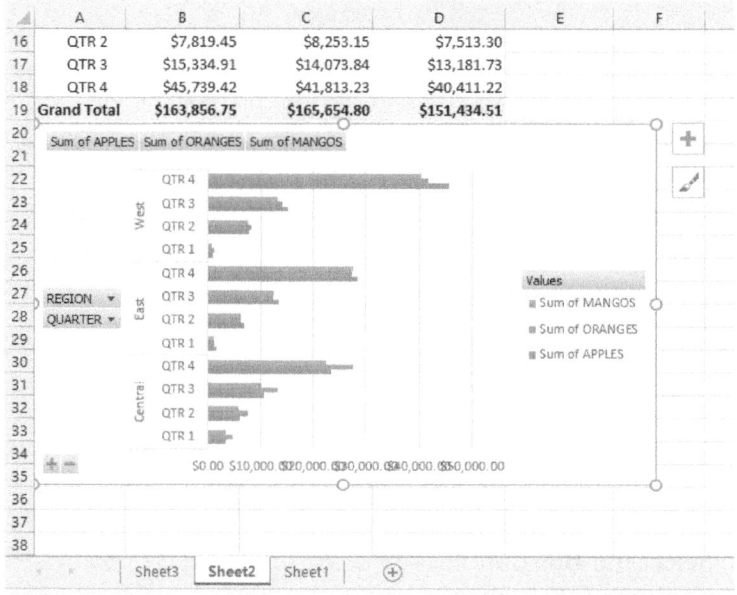

Fig. 3.16: Chart dragged below the Pivot Table report

6. From the **PivotChart Tools** Ribbon select the tab **Design** and under **Chart Styles** select a new style (Fig. 3.17):

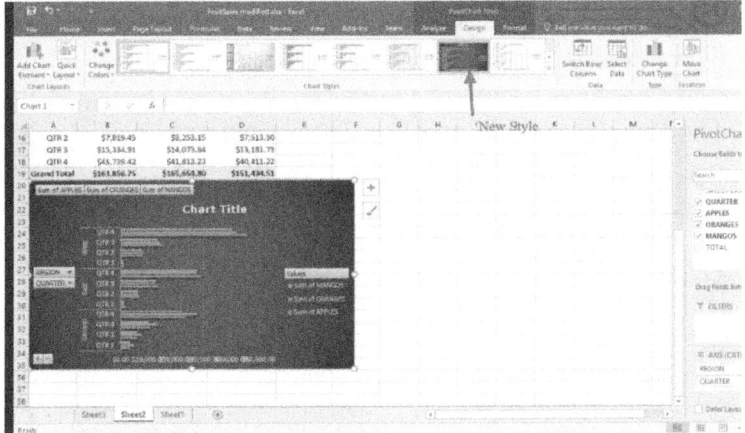

Fig. 3.17: Selecting new style under Chart Styles

7. If the chart title is hidden, you can reveal it by clicking on the **+** sign on the top right corner of the chart and then checking the **Chart Title** box under **Chart Elements** (see Fig. 3.18).

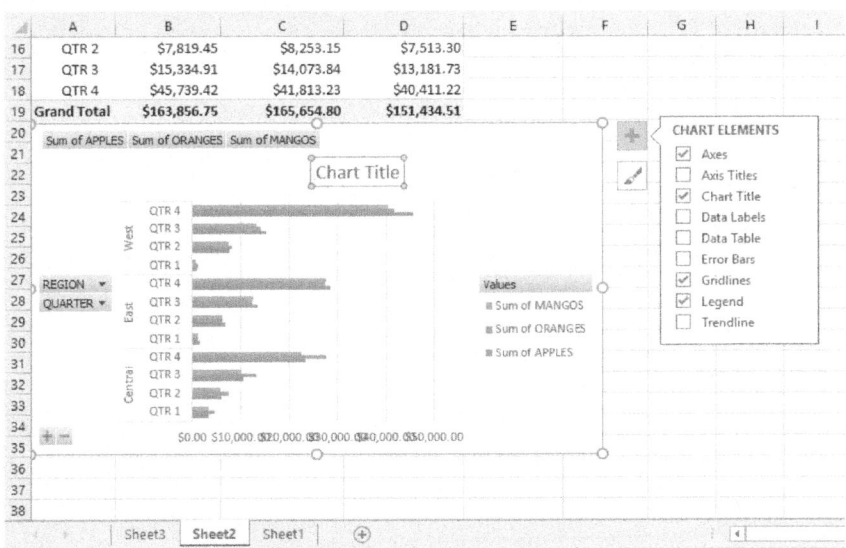

Fig. 3.18: Selecting the Chart Title

8. Edit the Chart Title by clicking inside the field, change text to "**Fruit Sales By Region & Quarter 2017**".

9. **Optional step**: To hide any of the Field buttons, right-click over it and select the appropriate hide option.

The final Chart will look like that shown in Fig. 3.19.

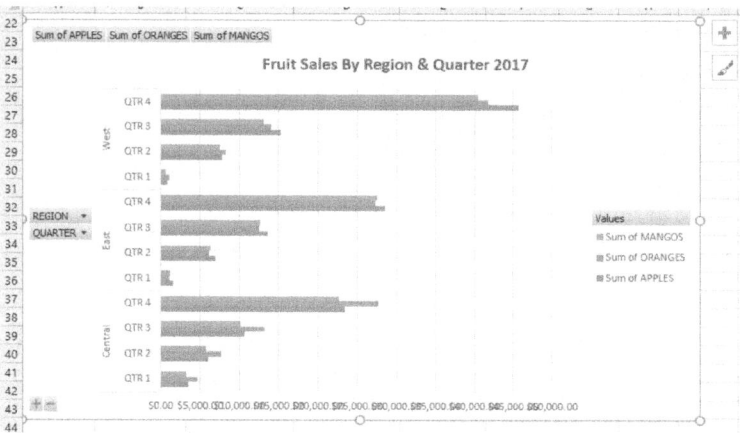

Fig. 3.19: Completed PivotTable Chart

Chapter 4: Slicers & Advanced Filtering

An additional tool within the Pivot Tables feature set are **Slicers**. Slicers are **graphical filters**, ideal for analysts or customers who like to examine data from many different perspectives. While filtering has always been a component of Pivot Tables, the introduction of the **Timeline Slicer** has been a welcome enhancement as it allows the user to quickly categorize *individual date values* into months, quarters, or years. There are two types of slicers:

1. **Timeline Slicers** available in **Excel®** versions **2013 & 2016**.
2. **Slicers** available in **Excel®** versions **2010, 2013, & 2016**.

Practice Project 1

Let us take a big practice project as our example this time. Supposing you are a Financial Analyst that supports a manufacturing company of aerospace parts. You have been asked to attend an impromptu sales meeting for regional managers. The agenda has not been determined, instead you have been asked to prepare the sales data for the last 12 months and answer questions as they arise. Since you're unsure of what the managers will ask, you decide to create a Pivot Table report with the slicers Category & Date.

For this prject, we will use the spreadsheet named **"AirplaneParts.xlsx"** which is inside the exercise folder you downloaded under the section "How to Use This Book".

Fig 4.0 shows a portion of this spreadsheet (truncated due to space limitation).

	A	B	C	D	E	F
1	REGION	NAME	CATEGORY	PART	EOM_DATE	QTY
2	Central	Graham, Peter	STRUCTURAL	Pressure Bulkheads	31 January 2017	8
3	Central	Graham, Peter	STRUCTURAL	Keel Beam	31 January 2017	11
4	Central	Graham, Peter	STRUCTURAL	Fuselage Panels	31 January 2017	13
5	Central	Graham, Peter	FUEL	Boost Pumps	31 January 2017	9
6	Central	Graham, Peter	FUEL	Transfer Valves	31 January 2017	5
7	Central	Graham, Peter	FUEL	Fuel S.O.V.	31 January 2017	6
8	Central	Graham, Peter	FUEL	Digital Fuel Flow System	31 January 2017	7
9	Central	Graham, Peter	FUEL	Fuel Quantity Indicator	31 January 2017	12
10	Central	Graham, Peter	FUEL	Fuel Flow Indicating	31 January 2017	7
11	Central	Graham, Peter	FUEL	Fuel Pressure Indicating	31 January 2017	4
12	Central	Graham, Peter	FUEL	Fuel Pump	31 January 2017	10
13	Central	Graham, Peter	FUEL	Engine Lubrication System	31 January 2017	6
14	Central	Graham, Peter	FUEL	Fuel Dump Fuel Hose	31 January 2017	9
15	Central	Graham, Peter	POWER	Lithium Battery	31 January 2017	4
16	Central	Graham, Peter	POWER	AC Generator-Alternator	31 January 2017	9
17	Central	Graham, Peter	POWER	Alternator/Generator Drive System	31 January 2017	4
18	Central	Graham, Peter	POWER	Fire Detection	31 January 2017	8
19	Central	Graham, Peter	POWER	Fire Protection	31 January 2017	13
20	Central	Graham, Peter	POWER	Overheat Detection	31 January 2017	4
21	Central	Graham, Peter	POWER	Smoke Detection	31 January 2017	11
22	Central	Graham, Peter	POWER	Extinguishing System	31 January 2017	8
23	Central	Graham, Peter	POWER	AC Inverter Phase Adapter	31 January 2017	8
24	Central	Graham, Peter	POWER	Fire Bottle-Fixed	31 January 2017	6
25	Central	Graham, Peter	POWER	AC Regulator	31 January 2017	7
26	Central	Graham, Peter	WING	Panels	31 January 2017	10

Fig. 4.0: AirplaneParts Spreadsheet

Timeline Slicer

Try to create the Pivot Table report by yourself to see the screenshot illustrations for steps 1 to 4. If necessary, *revise the previous chapters*, especially **chapter 3**. These are the same basic steps we followed in chapter 3 and we will follow them again:

1. Open the **AirplaneParts.xlsx** spreadsheet and highlight cells **A1:F3889** (i.e. **all** the cells - from cell **A1** to cell **F3889**).

Important Note: It is easy to highlight all the cells at once if you *first click on any cell* and then press **CTRL+A** on your keyboard.

2. From the Ribbon select **INSERT: PivotTable**.
3. Make sure the **New Worksheet** radio button is selected.
4. Click the **OK** button

A new tab will be created and the **PivotTable Fields** pane should appear on the **right side**.

5. Check/click the following fields:
a. **Region** (Rows section is filled automatically)
b. **Category** (Rows section is filled automatically)
c. **QTY** (Values section is filled automatically)

	A	B
1		
2		
3	Row Labels	Sum of QTY
4	⊟ Central	9768
5	FUEL	2842
6	POWER	2881
7	STRUCTURAL	721
8	WING	3324
9	⊟ East	9592
10	FUEL	2698
11	POWER	2897
12	STRUCTURAL	721
13	WING	3276
14	⊟ West	9312
15	FUEL	2538
16	POWER	2809
17	STRUCTURAL	893
18	WING	3072
19	Grand Total	28672
20		

Fig. 4.1: Pivot Table for AirplaneParts Spreadsheet

In order for a Timeline Slicer to work, all the data for that field must be **formatted as a date**. In this project, once we click the date field, **EOM_DATE** in **Excel® 2016** will create addition calendar options **Quarters & Years**.

6. Click the field **EOM_DATE**. As you can see, **Excel® 2016** has created fields for **Quarters & Years** (Fig. 4.2):

Start of section for Excel 2013 users only
If you are a users of **Excel 2013**, you must complete a few additional steps:

Select cell **A6**, right-click, and from the pop-up menu select **Group**....

When a prompt appears, press your **CTRL** button on your keyboard and select **Months**, **Quarters**, & **Years**. Click the **OK** button.
***End of section for Excel 2013 users only ***

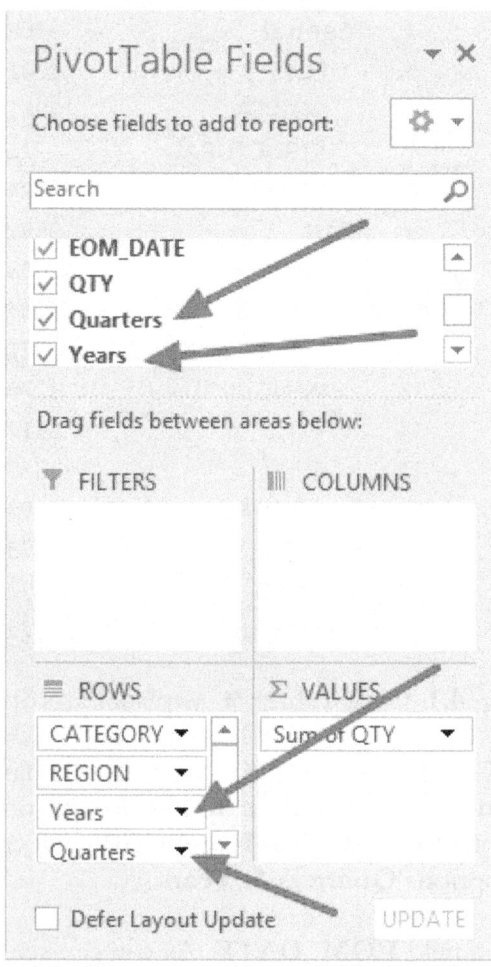

Fig. 4.2: Quarters & Years fields have been created

However, this type of display isn't very helpful. The Financial Analyst won't be able to quickly answer very many questions. Before adding our additional slicer, let's re-arrange the Pivot Table report to be more user friendly.

7. Uncheck fields **Years & Quarters**.
8. Drag the field **EOM_DATE** to the **Columns** area.

Note: how 'EOM_DATE' is now displaying as a month.

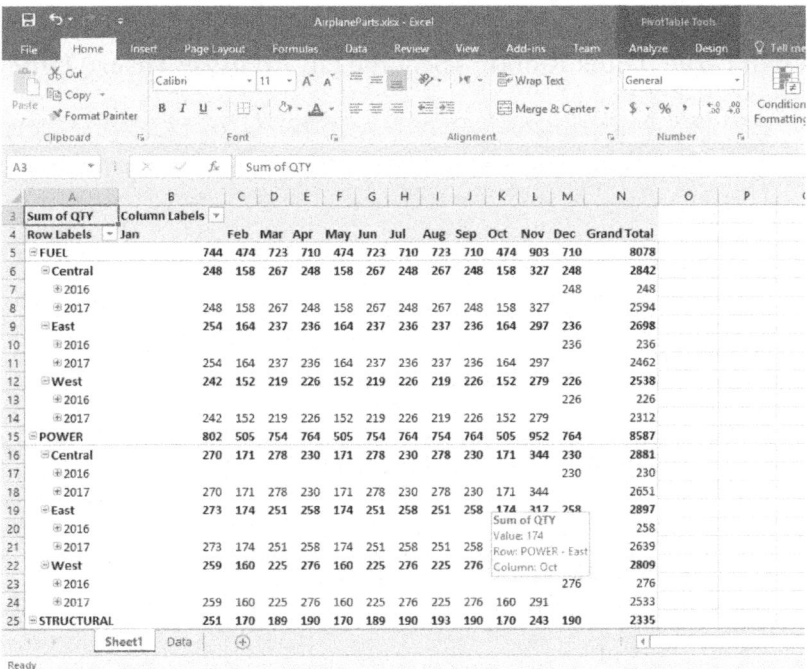

Fig. 4.3: EOM_DATE now displays as a month

9. Insert 8 blank rows above row 3 by right-clicking and selecting **insert > Entire row**. (Fig. 4.4):

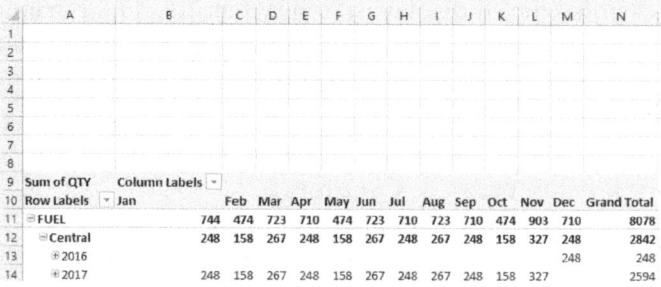

Fig. 4.4: 8 blank rows inserted above the report

10. With your cursor located inside the Pivot Table, from the **PivotTable Tools** Ribbon select the tab **Analyze: Insert Timeline**.

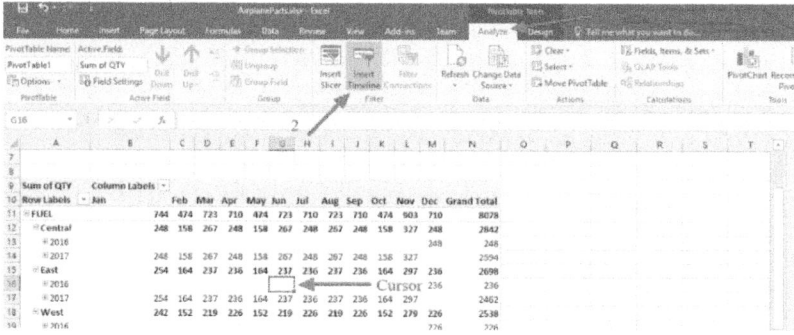

Fig. 4.5: Analyze: Insert Timeline tab selected

You'll receive the prompt shown in Fig. 4.6.
11. Click the **EOM_DATE** checkbox.
12. Click the **OK** button.

Fig. 4.6: EOM_DATE checkbox inside Insert Timelines prompt

13. The following **Timeline slicer** should now appear. Drag it to the area near cell **A1** above the report (inside the 8 blank rows).

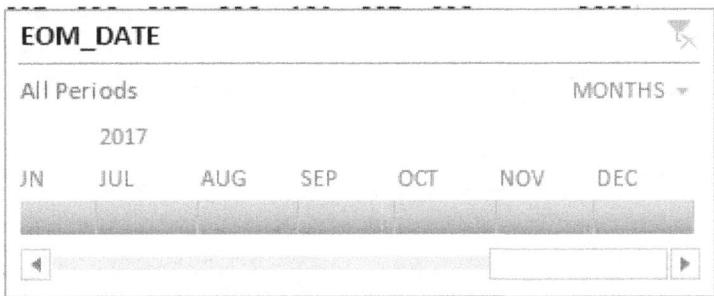

Fig. 4.7: Timeline slicer now appears

You can scroll horizontally, left or right. You may click the buttons under individual months to view how Pivot Table is updated instantly below (the counts change). For example, you may click **April 2017** to see totals change (See Fig. 4.8):

Excel Pivot Tables & Charts — - 43 -

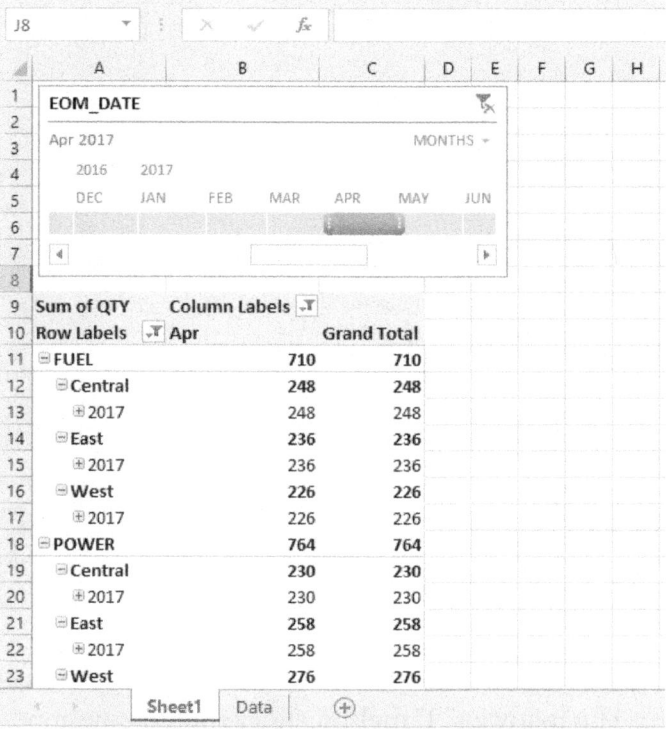

Fig. 4.8: Selecting months with buttons under the Timeline slicer

14. Change the Timeline Display from **Months** to **Quarters** by clicking on the **MONTHS** button near the top right corner. To remove all filters, click on the red cross on the top right corner (Fig. 4.9):

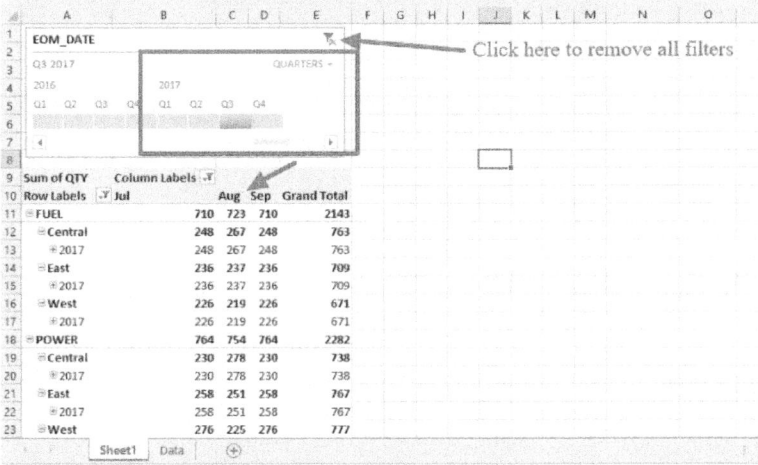

Fig. 4.9: Timeline Display changed from Months to Quarters

Slicer

We will continue this project by looking at the **Slicer** functionality.

1. With your cursor located inside the Pivot Table, from the **PivotTable Tools** Ribbon, select the tab **Analyze: Insert Slicer** (Fig. 4.10):

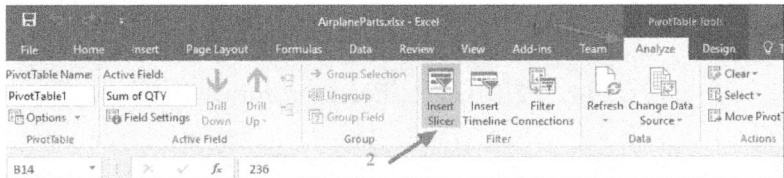

Fig. 4.10: Analyze: Insert Slicer tab selected

You'll receive the prompt shown in Fig. 4.11.
2. Click the **CATEGORY** checkbox.
3. Click the **OK** button.

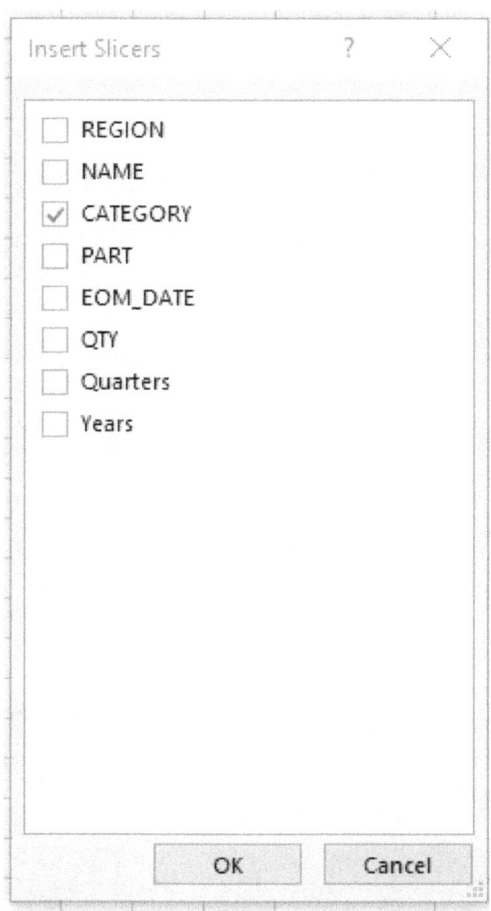

Fig. 4.11: Insert Slicers prompt window

4. The following slicer should now appear. Drag it to the area near cell **H1**.

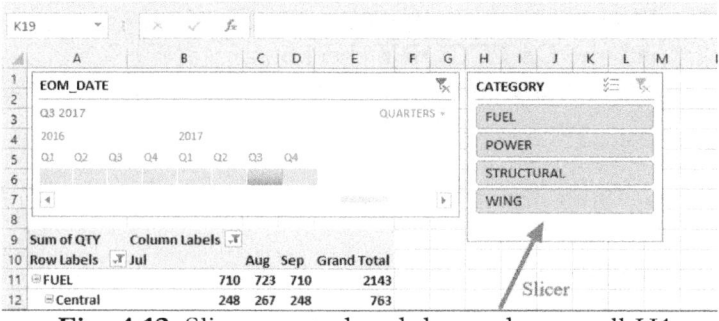

Fig. 4.12: Slicer created and dragged near cell H1

As a Financial Analyst, you may now answer all types of questions, with just a few clicks and without having to manually re-sort or add/remove formulas. Here are some examples:

- What are the total *Fuel* sales for **Feb 2017**?
- What are the **combined** sales for the *Structural & Wing* categories only?
- Provide the **Q4** sales for *Power*.

Additional Information

While having the date fields **Month**, **Quarter** and **Year** automatically be added to our Pivot Table fields list is helpful, there still may be times when you want to have the **individual dates** included in your report. To see the individual date values in our current project, place your cursor inside the Pivot Table and follow these steps:

1. From the **PivotTable Fields** pane uncheck fields **REGION** and **CATEGORY**.
2. Drag **EOM_DATE** from **Columns** to **Rows**.
3. From the Pivot Table, **right-click** over any of the month values.
4. From the pop-up menu, select **Ungroup**...

See Fig. 4.13:

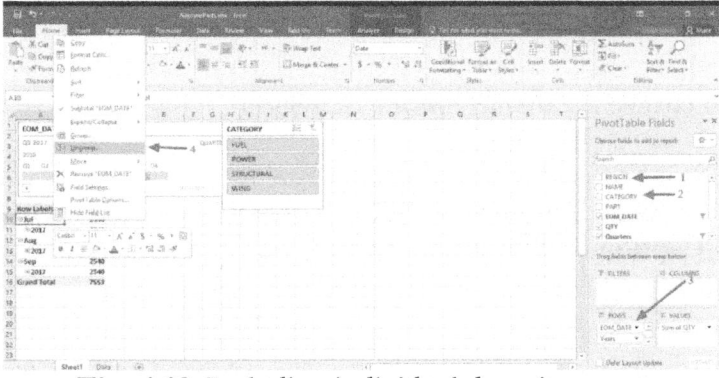

Fig. 4.13: Including individual dates in report

The individual dates should now be displayed:

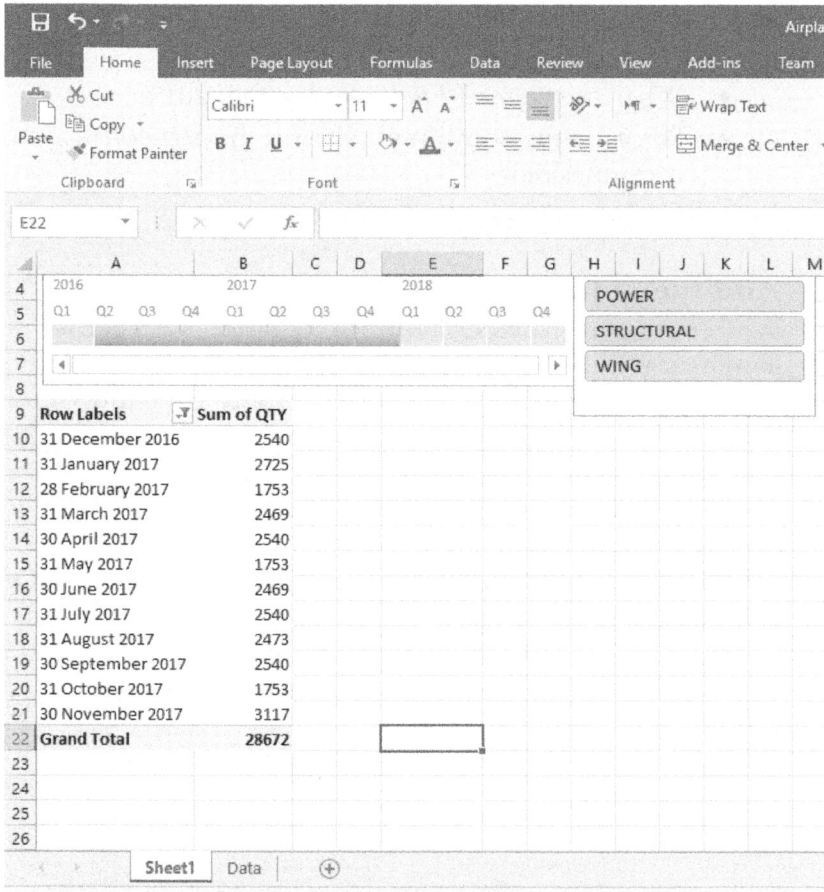

Fig. 4.14: Individual dates displayed in report

To change the *display name* of a Slicer:

1. Select the Slicer
2. From the **Timeline** or **Slicer Tools** Ribbon, under **Options** go to **Caption** or **Timeline Caption** and enter a new name (Fig. 4.15):

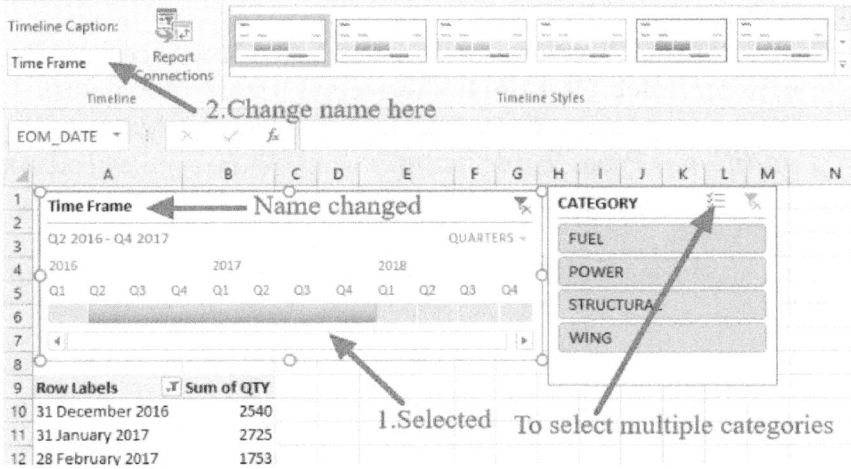

Fig. 4.15: Display name changed

To change the color format of a Slicer:

1. Select the Slicer
2. From the **Timeline** or **Slicer Tools** Ribbon under **Options** go to **Timeline Styles** or **Slicer Styles** and select a new color scheme (Fig. 4.16):

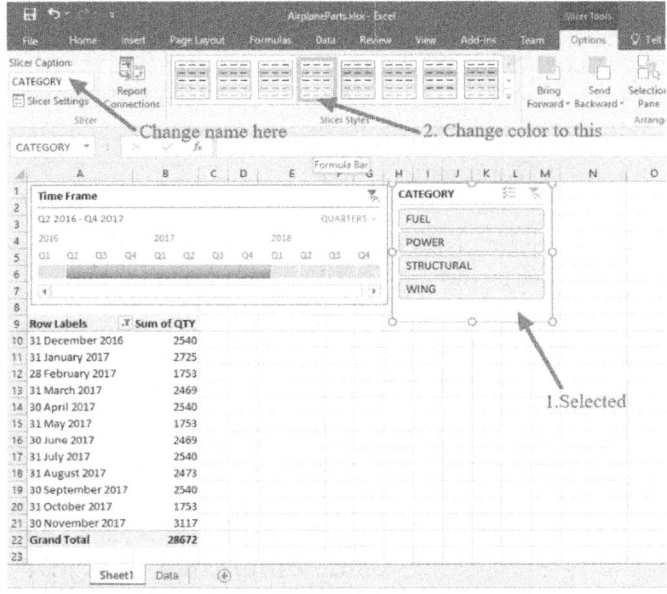

Fig. 4.16: Clor format changed

Advanced Filtering

In the first part of our project, we reviewed how Slicers may be used for **quick filtering**. In this section we will take another look at our project. We will demonstrate how to employ *additional Pivot Table features* which allow us to extend our analysis by *specifying conditions*.

So, supposing in our **AirplaneParts** spreadsheet, we wanted to know:

1. The **top 10** airplane parts sold by category?
2. The **bottom 10** airplane parts sold by category?
3. The **top 10** airplane parts sold by Quarter?
4. How many parts sold more than 800 in quantity?

If you're familiar with Excel's conditional formatting capabilities, this is very similar in Pivot Tables. Let's walk through it and show how this functionality may be utilized. We follow the same steps like before. So complete steps 1 to 4 on your own.

1. Unzip **a new copy of** your zipped project folder. Open the AirplaneParts.xlsx spreadsheet in your Excel application and highlight cells **A1:F3889**.
2. From the Ribbon select **INSERT: PivotTable**.
3. Ensure the **New Worksheet** radio button is selected.
4. Click the **OK** button.

A new tab will be created and the **PivotTable Fields** pane should appear on the **right side**.

5. Click the following fields:
   a. **Part** (Rows section is filled automatically).
   b. **Category** (Rows section is filled automatically).
   c. **QTY** (Values section is filled automatically).

6. Click the drop-down arrow of **Row Labels** cell (**A4**).
7. From the menu select **Value Filters** then **Top 10**.

See Fig. 4.17 for steps 5 to 7:

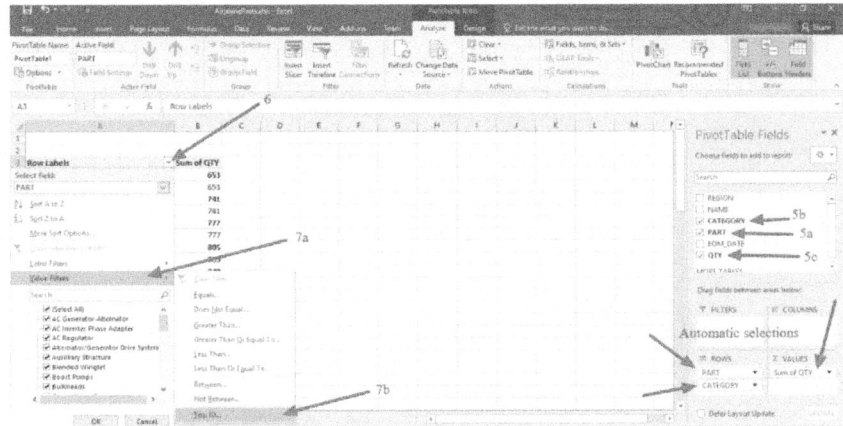

Fig. 4.17: Selecting Top 10 Value Filter

8. The prompt in Fig. 4.18 will appear. Note that you may change **10** to any other number you would like to see, say **5**. You may also change **Top** to **Bottom**. Finally, click the **OK** button.

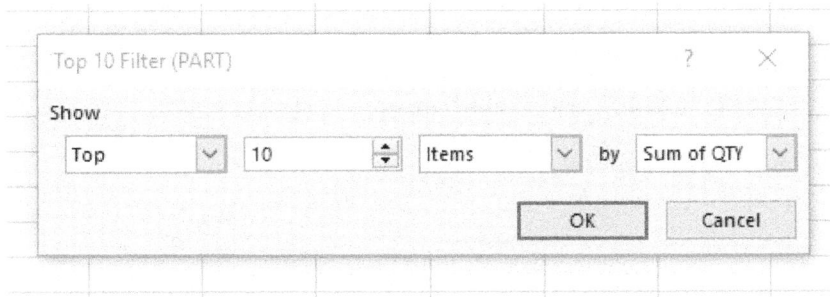

Fig. 4.18: Top 10 Value Filter prompt window

The following Fig. 4.19 will be the result.

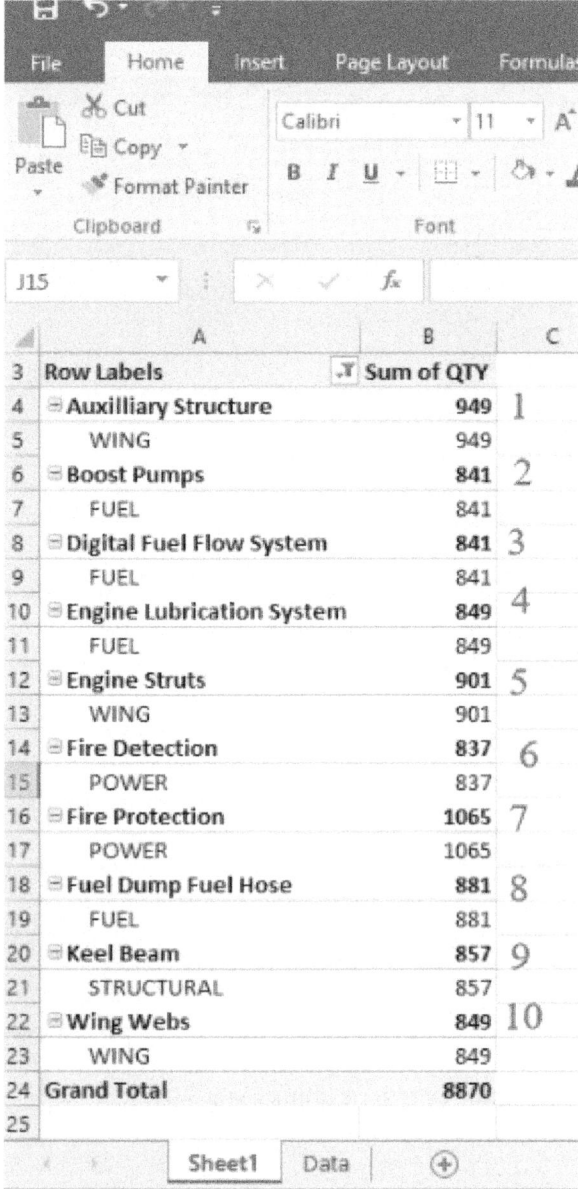

Fig. 4.19: Result for Top 10 Value Filter

Lastly, to show how many parts sold more than 800 in quantity, follow the same steps shown in Fig 4.17 above but select **Greater Than** in step 2 below:

1. Click the drop-down arrow of **Row Labels**.
2. From the menu select **Value Filters** then **Greater Than**...
3. The following prompt will appear, enter the number **800** in the field after the dropdown box **is greater than**.
4. Click the **OK** button.

See Fig. 4.20

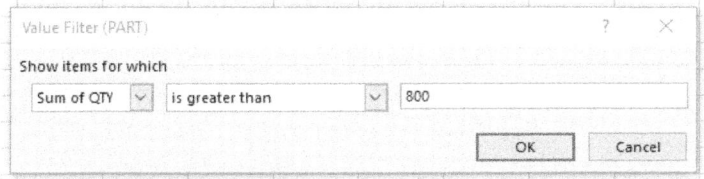

Fig. 4.20: Result for Greater Than Value Filter

Fig. 4.21 will be the result (Figure is truncated at the bottom because of space limitation):

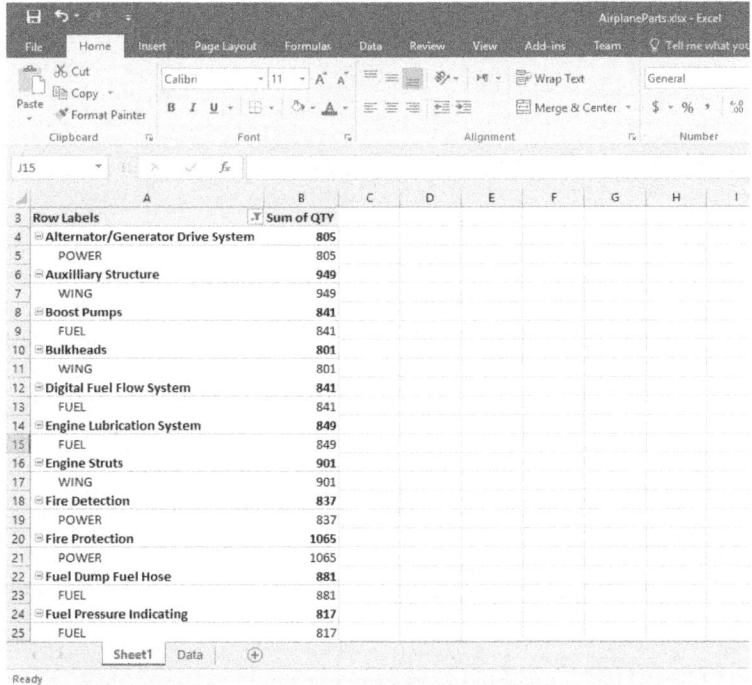

Fig. 4.21: Result for "more than 800 in quantity"

Excel Pivot Tables & Charts   - 53 -

To remove a filter, follow these steps (similar to above steps):

1. Click the drop-down arrow of **Row Labels**.
2. From the menu select **Clear Filter From**...

Chapter 5: Calculations in Pivot Tables

Calculated Fields

As demonstrated in previous chapters, Pivot Tables have many powerful analysis features already built-in, however the type of work you perform may require more complex or technical types of calculations than those included in the standard set of Pivot Table **Value Field Settings**. This is when the ability to insert your own **Calculated Fields** is particularly helpful.

For example, let us say you are responsible for analyzing your company's sales location plan vs. actual. In addition to this you also determine if a store is eligible for a bonus and if they earned a bonus, what the bonus amount to be paid is.

You perform this type of analysis on a regular basis and it is the type of business, where some *stores may close and others open from month-to-month*.

You need to report:

1. The monthly sales dollar variance -/+ plan vs. actual by location.
2. The monthly percent variance -/+ plan vs. actual by location.
3. If the store is eligible for a bonus, based on actual sales greater than 1.5% over planned sales.
4. If the store earned a bonus, the dollar amount owed to each location, which is 2% of that store's actual sales.

Practice Project 2

We will use the spreadsheet named "**StoresSales.xlsx**" in the exercise folder that you downloaded under the section "How to Use This Book" to perform our analysis, step by step.

Fig 5.0 below shows a portion of this spreadsheet.

	A	B	C	D	E	F	G	H	I
1	Location	Month	Planned Sales	Actual Sales		Data for adding new locations			
2	AAA	Jan	406	414		AAA	Apr	432	450
3	BBB	Jan	332	329		BBB	Apr	338	329
4	CCC	Jan	496	526		CCC	Apr	509	526
5	DDD	Jan	152	156		DDD	Apr	155	150
6	EEE	Jan	178	173		FFF	Apr	191	170
7	AAA	Feb	415	427		GGG	Apr	181	170
8	BBB	Feb	346	342					
9	CCC	Feb	551	595					
10	DDD	Feb	175	184					
11	EEE	Feb	173	183					
12	AAA	Mar	424	416					
13	BBB	Mar	360	363					
14	CCC	Mar	612	648					
15	DDD	Mar	202	207					
16	EEE	Mar	168	163					
17									

Fig. 5.0: StoresSales.xlsx Spreadsheet

Adding A Basic Calculated Field

Just like you did in the last chapter, first create a basic Pivot Table report by yourself by following steps 1 to 4 below:

1. Open the StoreSales.xlsx spreadsheet and highlight *columns* **A:D**
2. From the Ribbon select **INSERT: PivotTable**.
3. Select the **New Worksheet** radio button.
4. Click the **OK** button.

A new tab will be created and the 'PivotTable Fields' pane should appear on the **right side**.

5. Select the following fields:
a. **Location** (Column section is filled automatically).
b. **Month** (Rows section is filled automatically).
c. **Planned Sales** and **Actual Sales** (Values section is filled automatically).

Please note: When adding the QTY fields, it will default to **Count of QTY**. Change it to **Sum**.

d. **Values** (drag this field to the Rows section, making sure it is *below the Month field*). See Fig. 5.1:

Excel Pivot Tables & Charts   - 56 -

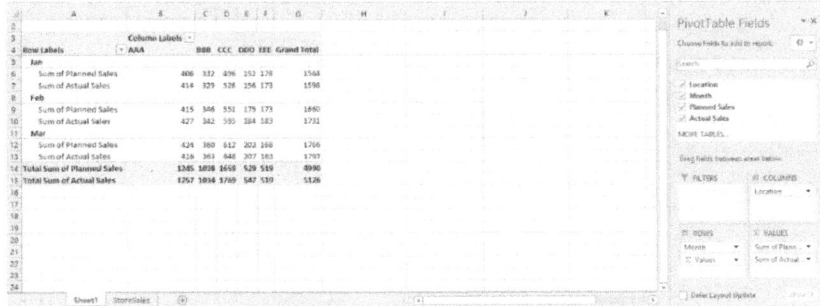

Fig. 5.1: Updated PivotTable

6. Change the text in cell **A4** to **MONTH**.
7. Change the text in cell **B3** to **LOCATION**.
8. Click on **Sum of Planned Sales** in the Values section. Select **Value Field Settings** (see Fig 5.2):

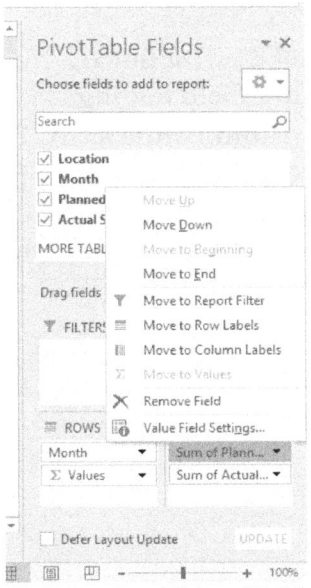

Fig. 5.2: Selecting Value Field Settings in the PivotTable Fields

- Inside the **Value Field Settings** window, change **Custom Name** to **PLN SLS**.
- Click on **Number Format** to open the **Format Cells** window where you can change to a *currency* of your choice ($ for example). Click **OK** to close each of the two windows in turn. See Fig. 5.3:

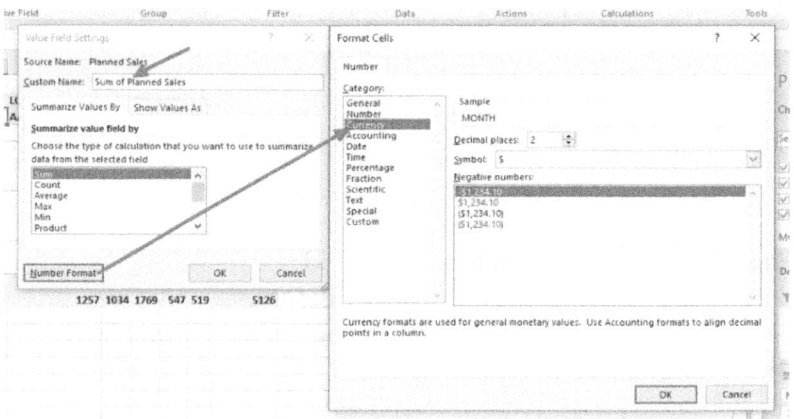

Fig. 5.3: Changing Custom Name and Currency

9. Repeat step 8 but now for **Sum of Actual Sales** in the Values section. Select **Value Field Settings**.
- Change **Custom Name** to **ACT SLS**.
- Click on **Number Format** to open the **Format Cells** window where you can change to a *currency* of your choice ($ for example). Click **OK** to close each of the two windows in turn.

The Pivot Table should now look similar to Fig. 5.4:

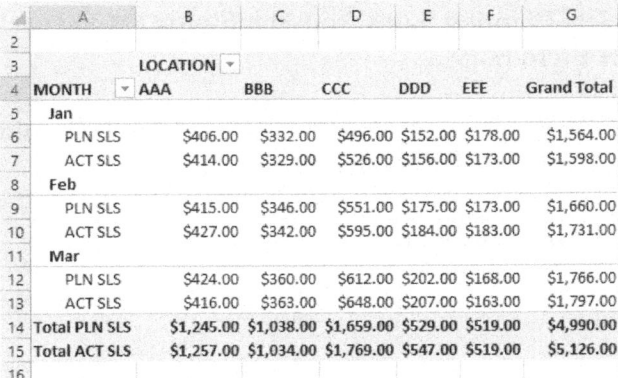

Fig. 5.4: New updated PivotTable

To add our first calculated field showing the sales dollar variance -/+ plan vs. actual.

10. From the **PivotTable Tools** Ribbon select the tab **Analyze**.
11. Click the **Fields, Items & Sets** drop-down box. See Fig. 5.5.
12. Select **Calculated Field**...

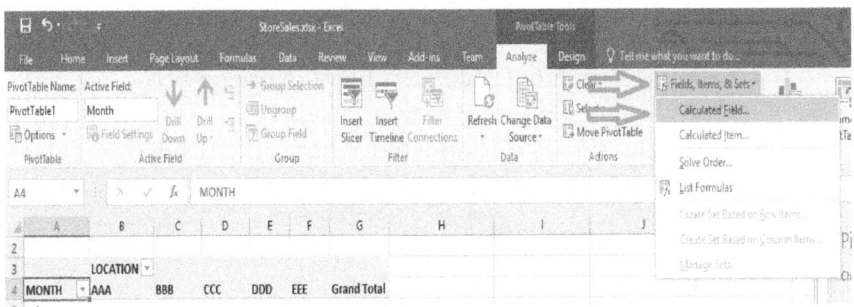

Fig. 5.5: Selecting Calculated Field…

A dialogue box similar to Fig. 5.6 below will appear:

13. In the **Name:** field, enter **Dollars -/+ plan vs actual**.
14. In the **Formula:** field delete the zero '0', but leave the equal '=' sign.
15. Select **Actual Sales** from the **Fields** list and click the **Insert Field** button.
16. Add the minus '-' symbol in the **Formula:** field after **Actual Sales**.

17. Select **Planned Sales** from the **Fields** list and click the **Insert Field** button.

The following formula should now be in the **Formula:** field = 'ACTUAL SALES' - PLAN SALES'.

18. Click the **OK** button.

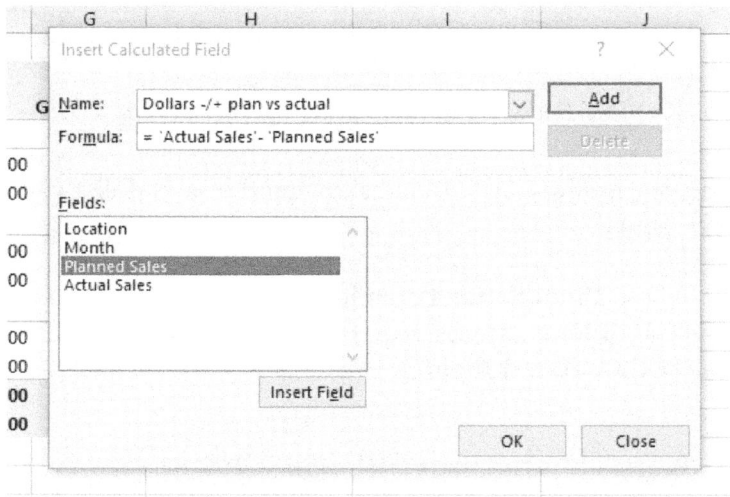

Fig. 5.6: Calculated Field dialogue box

Fig. 5.7 below shows our updated PivotTable results:

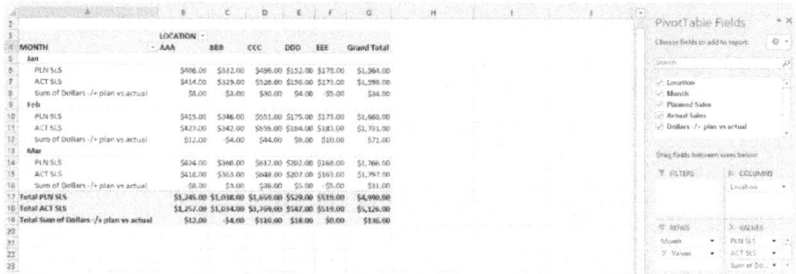

Fig. 5.7: Updated PivotTable results

Next, we'll add the calculated field for the **percent variance -/+ plan vs. actual**. The steps to follow are similar to those you already performed above.

19. Repeat steps 10 to 12 from above.
20. In the **Name:** field enter **Percent -/+ plan vs actual**.
21. In the **Formula:** field delete the zero **'0'**, but leave the equal **'='** sign.
22. Add the below formula to the **Formula:** field
(**'Actual Sales'-'Planned Sales')/ 'Planned Sales'**.
23. Click the **OK** button.

Fig. 5.8 below shows our updated PivotTable results:

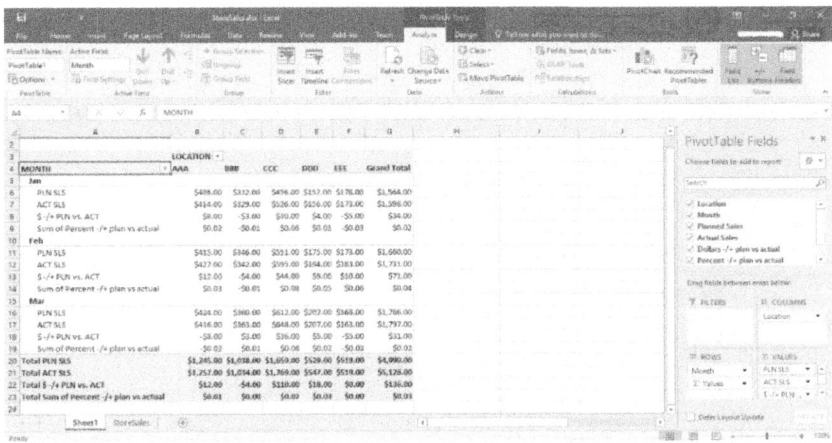

Fig. 5.8: Newly updated PivotTable results

Let us now **format our report to improve readability**. Follow steps 1 to 14 below. They are very similar to the steps you already performed above. If at any time you discovered you have already performed any of the steps below, you can just skip them:

1. In the PivotTable Fields list, in the VALUES section, click the drop-down box for **Sum of Dollars -/+ plan vs actual**. (Scroll down a little inside the box if you do not see it).
2. Select the **Value Field Settings**.
3. Change the **Custom Name:** to **$ -/+ PLN vs. ACT**.
4. Click the **OK** button.
5. In the PivotTable Fields list, in the VALUES section, click the drop-down box for **Sum of Percent -/+ plan vs actual**.
6. Select the **Value Field Settings**.
7. Change the **Custom Name:** to **% -/+ PLN vs. ACT**.

8. Click the **Number Format** to change the **Percentage** format to 1 decimal place (Use the scroll buttons or just type 1 inside the box).
9. Click the **OK** button for each dialogue box.
10. Inside the Pivot Table, click the drop-down box for **MONTH** (cell **A4**) and select **Label Filters** then **Does Not Equal**.
11. A small window titled **Label Filter (Month)** will appear (Fig. 5.9). When prompted, enter (blank), this method will ensure when we refresh the data, no blank rows & columns will appear, but our new locations will. Click **OK**.

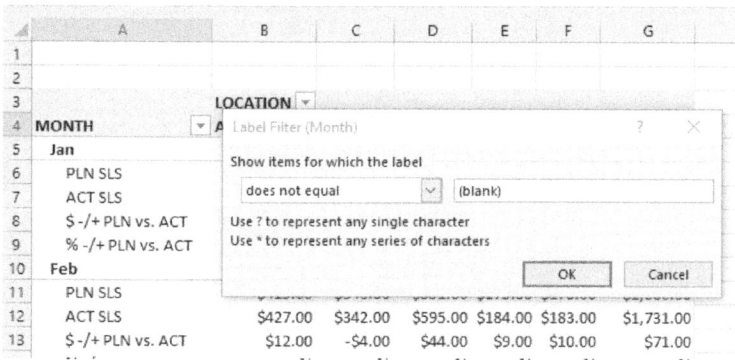

Fig. 5.9: Filling the Label Filter (Month) window

12. From the **PivotTable Tools** Ribbon select the tab **Design**.
13. Select **PivotTable Style** of your choice.
14. Click the checkbox **Banded Columns**.
See Fig. 5.10.

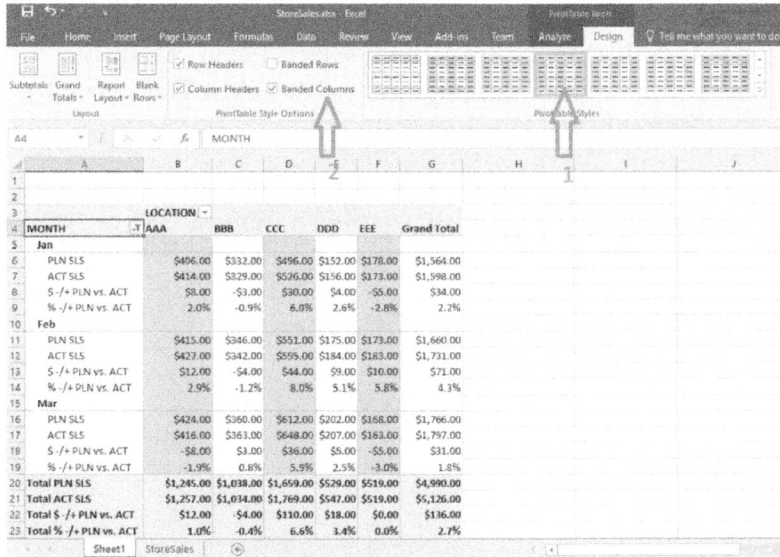

Fig. 5.10: PivotTable Style and Banded Columns selected

Now let's examine how our results change when we **add** or **remove** locations.

1. Return to the **StoreSales** worksheet by clicking on it.
2. Copy cells **F2:I7** and paste (CTRL+V) into in cell **A17**. See Fig. 5.11.

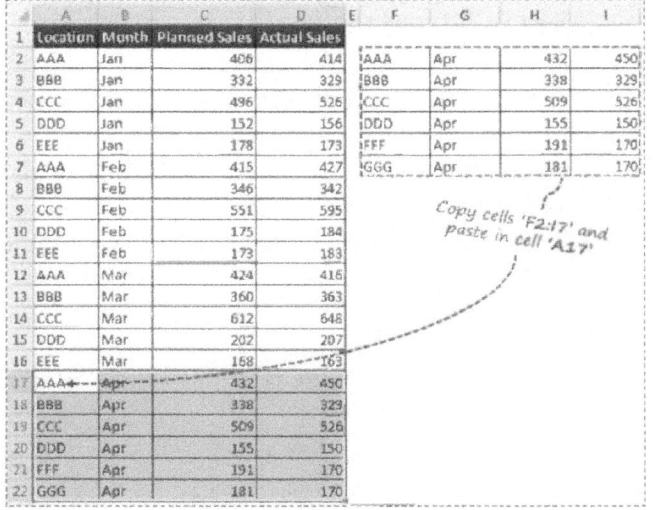

Fig. 5.11: Copying cells F2:I7 and pasting inside cell A17

3. Return to the **Pivot Tables** tab (Sheet1), from the **PivotTable Tools** Ribbon select the tab **Analyze**.
4. Click the down-pointing arrow below **Refresh**. Then click **Refresh All**. Fig. 5.12.

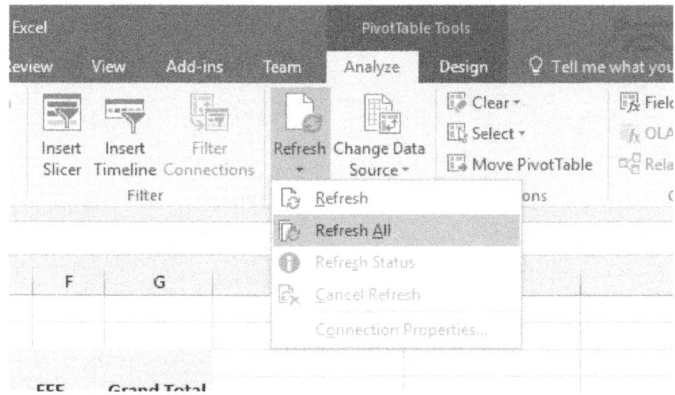

Fig. 5.12: Selecting Refresh All

Removing Or Changing Calculated Fields

To remove or change a calculated field follow these simple steps (similar to the steps you performed before):

1. From the **PivotTable Tools** Ribbon select the tab **Analyze**.
2. Click the **Fields, Items & Sets** drop-down box.
3. Select **Calculated Field**...

The Calculated dialogue box in Fig. 5.13 will appear.

4. In the **Name:** drop-down box select the calculated field you would like to change or remove.
5. Click appropriate button, either **Modify** or **Delete**.

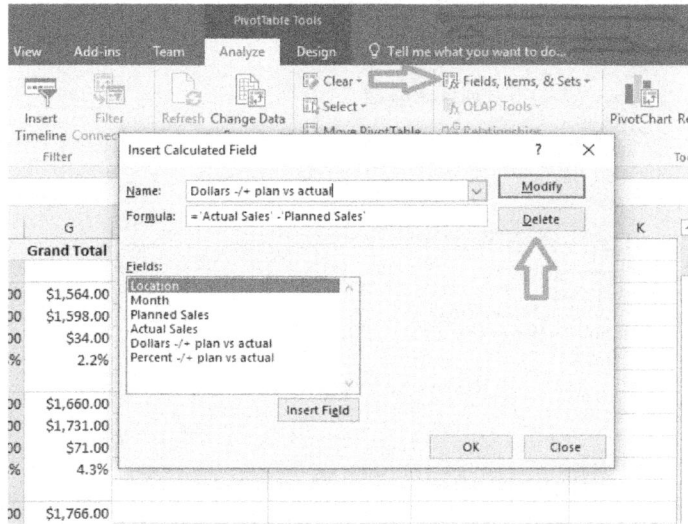

Fig. 5.13: Calculated Field dialogue box

Inserting Logic Fields (if...then)

We will need to add 2 additional calculated fields, in order to answer the following questions:

• Is the store eligible for a bonus based on actual sales greater than 1.5% over planned sales?
• If the store earned a bonus, what is the dollar amount owed to that location? This is calculated as 2% of that store's actual sales.

The 2 calculated fields needed are:
1. **Location Eligibility Amount** to calculate what is 1.5% over the planned sales for each location?
2. **Bonus Award** the dollar amount owed, if they earned the bonus, what is 2% of actual sales for that location?

Location_Eligibility_Amt formula:

='Planned Sales'+('Planned Sales'*0.015)

Excel Pivot TABLES & Charts

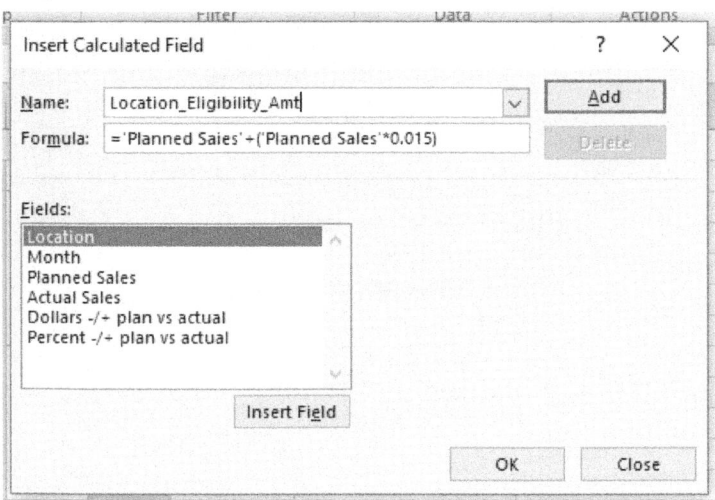

Fig. 5.14: Calculated Field for Location_Eligibility_Amt

Bonus_Award formula:

=IF('Actual Sales '>Location_Eligibility_Amt,('Actual Sales '*0.02),0)

Chapter 6: Customizing Pivot Tables

In this chapter we look at how you can use several powerful settings available in Excel 2016 to tweak pivot tables. Such tweaks range from doing cosmetic changes to changing the underlying calculation that is used in the pivot table. You may have noticed that some customization has already been touched in the last chapter.

Even though pivot tables are an extremely speedy way of summarizing data, the pivot table defaults are sometimes not exactly what we need. For such cases, many powerful settings can be used to tweak pivot tables.

In Excel 2016, controls for customize=ing a pivot table can be found in myriad places such as the **Analyze** tab, **Field Settings** dialog **Design** tab, **Data Field Settings** dialog, **PivotTable Options** dialog, and some context menus.

These following are some functional areas where pivot table customization is done:

- Making major cosmetic changes such as using pivot table **styles** to format any pivot table very quickly.
- Making minor cosmetic changes such as changing blanks to **0's** (zeros), adjusting a **number format**, and **renaming** a field. Trying to correct all these defaults in each pivot table that you create can be very annoying.
- Making layout changes such as Comparing 3 possible layouts, showing or hiding subtotals and totals, and repeating row labels.
- Making summary calculations such as changing from **Sum** to **Count**, **Min**, **Max**, and more. In a pivot table where the default is **Count of Revenue**, you can change itto **Sum of Revenue** instead.
- Performing advanced calculations such as using settings to show data as a running total. This is also true of percent of total, rank, percent of parent item, and many more.

Some of the above customizations were already applied to the project done (Practice project 2) in chapter 5. A few more will now be discussed below.

Making Major Cosmetic Changes
You need to make a few changes to almost every pivot table to make it easier to understand and interpret. Fig. 6.0 shows a typical pivot table.

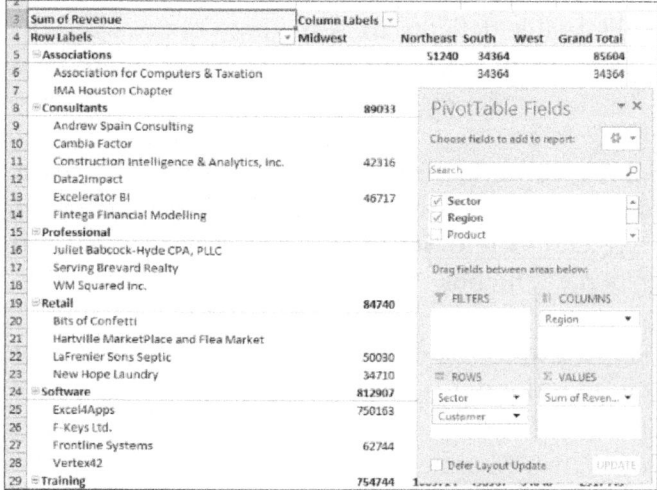

Fig. 6.0: A Typical Pivot table

Using a Table Style to Restore Gridlines
The default Fig. 6.0 is a pivot table layout having no gridlines. It is too plain. Fortunately, a table style can be applied. Choose any table style that you like.

Follow these steps to apply a table style:

1. Ensure that the active cell is within the pivot table.
2. From the ribbon, select the **Design** tab. Three arrows appear at the right side of the **PivotTable Style** gallery.
3. Click the bottom arrow to open the complete gallery, as shown in Fig. 6.1:

Fig. 6.1: Complete PivotTable Style gallery

4. From the drop-down menu, choose any style different from the first style. Styles near the bottom tend to have more formatting.
5. Select the check box for **Banded Rows** to the left of the PivotTable Styles gallery. This draws light-style gridlines and adds dark-style row stripes.

The style you choose from the gallery does not matter. There are 84 other styles that are better than the default one.

Making Minor Cosmetic Changes
Adding Thousands Separators in Number Formatting.

If you have ever formatted your underlying data, you might be expecting that the pivot table will include some of this formatting. Unfortunately, it is not so. Even if you formatted your underlying data fields with a certain numeric format, the default pivot table will present values that are formatted with a general format.

Let us use Fig. 6.0 as an example. As you can see, the numbers are in the thousands or tens of thousands. Normally, you would expect to have a thousands separator and probably no decimal places. Even though the original data possesses a numeric format, the general style in which the pivot table routinely formats your numbers is ugly.

There are 3 ways to reach the **Value Field Settings** dialog:

- Right-click a number in the Values area of the pivot table and select **Value Field Settings**.
- Click the drop-down to the right of the **Sum of Revenue** field in the areas of the PivotTable Fields list and then select **Value Field Settings** from the context menu.
- Select any cell in the Values area of the pivot table. From the **Analyze** tab, select **Field Settings** from the **Active Field group**.

As shown in Fig. 6.2, the Value Field Settings dialog is displayed. To change the numeric format, click on the **Number Format** button on the lower-left corner of the box.

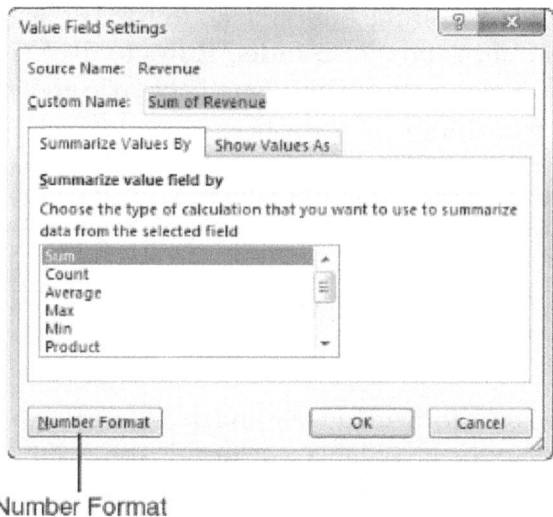

Number Format

Fig. 6.2: Value Field Settings dialogue box

In the **Format Cells** dialogue box of Fig. 6.3, select any built-in number format or choose a custom one. For instance, you can select Currency, as shown in Fig. 6.3.

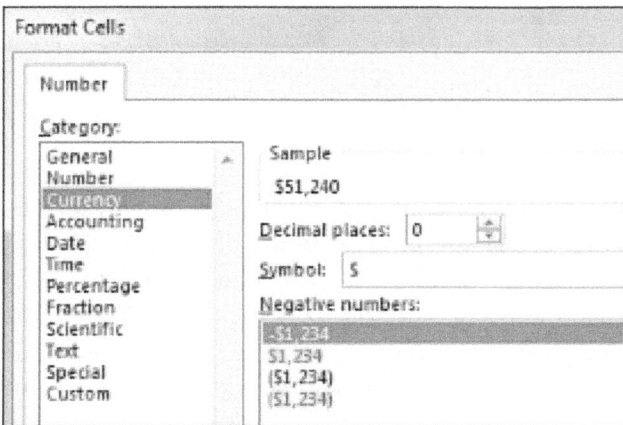

Fig. 6.3: Format Cells dialogue box

Please note that Excel 2016 offers a live preview feature for several format settings. However, the Format Cells dialogue does not offer any such preview. To see your changes, you must assign the number format, close the Format dialogue box, and then close the Value Field Settings dialogue box.

Chapter 7: Using VBA Macro Language to Create Pivot Tables

Introduction to VBA

Microsoft Excel introduced a powerful new **macro language** called **Visual Basic for Applications (VBA)**. Every version of Excel produced since 1993 has had a copy of the powerful VBA language hiding behind the worksheets. VBA enables you to perform steps that you normally perform in Excel quickly and flawlessly. I have seen a VBA program change a process that would take days each month and turn it into a single button click and a minute of processing time.

Why Use Macros with Your Pivot Table Reports?

Imagine that you could be in multiple locations at one time, with multiple clients at one time, helping them with their pivot table reports. Suppose you could help multiple clients refresh their data, extract top 20 records, group by months, or sort by revenue. The fact is you can do just that by using Excel macros.

A **macro** is a series of keystrokes that have been recorded and saved. After saved, the macro can be played back on command. In other words, you can record your actions in a macro, save the macro, and then allow your clients to play back your actions with the touch of a button. It would be as though you were there with them! This functionality is exceptionally useful when you're distributing pivot table reports.

For example, suppose you want to give your clients the option of grouping their pivot table report by month, quarter, or year. Although the process of grouping can be technically performed by anyone, some of your clients might not have a clue how to do it. In this case, you could record a macro to group by month, a macro to group by quarter, and a macro to group by year. Then, you could create three buttons, one for each macro. In the end, your clients, having little experience with pivot tables, need only to click a button to group their pivot table report.

A major benefit of using macros with your pivot table reports is the power you can give your clients to easily perform pivot table actions that they would not normally be able to perform on their own, empowering them to more effectively analyze the data you provide.

Recording Your First Macro

Look at the pivot table in Fig. 7.0. You know that you can refresh this pivot table (or any other pivot tables you created earlier in this book) by right-clicking inside the pivot table and selecting **Refresh**. Now, if you were to record your actions with a macro while you refreshed your pivot table, you, or anyone else, could replicate your actions and refresh this pivot table by running the macro.

	A	B
1	Region	(All)
2		
3	Row Labels	Sum of Sales_Amount
4	ACASCO Corp.	$675
5	ACECUL Corp.	$593
6	ACEHUA Corp.	$580
7	ACOPUL Corp.	$675
8	ACORAR Corp.	$2,232
9	ACSBUR Corp.	$720
10	ADACEC Corp.	$345
11	ADADUL Corp.	$690
12	ADANAS Corp.	$345
13	ADCOMP Corp.	$553
14	ADDATI Corp.	$379
15	ADDOUS Corp.	$5,209
16	ADEARM Corp.	$357

Fig. 7.0: A sample PivotTable

This basic pivot table can easily be refreshed by right-clicking and selecting **Refresh**, but if you recorded your actions with a macro, you could also refresh this pivot table simply by *running the macro*.

The first step in recording a macro is to initiate the **Record Macro** dialog box. Select the **Developer** tab on the Ribbon, and then select **Record Macro**.

Important Tip: Can't find the **Developer** tab on the Ribbon? Click the **File** tab on the Ribbon, and then select the **Options** selection. This opens the **Excel Options** dialog box, where you click **Customize Ribbon**. In the **ListBox** to the far right, you select the **Developer** check box. Selecting this option enables the **Developer** tab.

When the Record Macro dialog box activates, you can fill in a few key pieces of information about the macro:
- Macro Name: Enter a name for your macro. You should generally enter a name that describes the action being performed.
- Shortcut Key: You can enter any letter into this input box. That letter becomes part of a set of keys on your keyboard that can be pressed (in conjunction with the Ctrl key) to play back the macro. This is optional.
- Store Macro In: Specify where you want the macro to be stored. If you are distributing your pivot table report, you should select **This Workbook** so that the macro is available to your clients.
- Description: In this input box, you can enter a few words that give more detail about the macro.

Because this macro refreshes your pivot table when it is played, name your macro **RefreshData**. Also assign a shortcut key of **R**. Notice that the dialog box gives you a full key of **Ctrl+Shift+R**. Keep in mind that you use the full key to play your macro after it is created. Be sure to store the macro in **This Workbook**. Click **OK** to continue. When this is done, your dialog box should look like the one shown in Fig. 7.1:

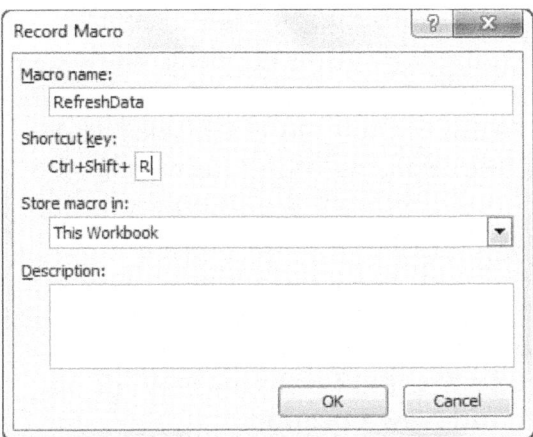

Fig. 7.1: Record Macro dialogue box

When you click **OK** in the **Record Macro** dialog box, you initiate the recording process. At this point, any action you perform is being recorded by Excel. In that case, you want to record the process of refreshing your pivot table.

Right-click anywhere inside the pivot table, and then select **Refresh**. After you have refreshed your pivot table, you can stop the recording process by going up to the **Developer** tab and selecting the **Stop Recording** button.

Congratulations! You have just recorded your first macro. You can now play your macro by pressing **Ctrl+Shift+R**.

Important Note on Macro Security: You should be aware that when you record a macro yourself, your macro runs fine on your PC with no security restrictions. However, when you distribute workbooks that contain macros, your clients have to let Excel know that your workbook is not a security risk, thus enabling your macros to run.

Indeed, you should note that the any file that comes with micros with this book does not run unless you tell Excel to enable the macros within.

The best way to do this is to use the workbook in a trusted location, a directory that is deemed a safe zone where only trusted workbooks are placed. A trusted location enables you and your clients to run a macro-enabled workbook with no security restrictions, as long as the workbook is in that location.

To set up a trusted location, follow these steps:

1. Select the **Macro Security** button on the **Developer** tab. This activates the **Trust Center** dialogue box.
2. Select the **Trusted Locations** button.
3. Select **Add New Location**.
4. Click **Browse** to specify the directory to be considered a trusted location.

After you specify a trusted location, Click **OK** on each box to close them. Henceforth, all workbooks opened from that location are, by default, opened with macros enabled.

In the next section, you will go beyond recording macros. You will learn *"Using VBA to Create Pivot Tables"*. You will know how to utilize VBA to create powerful, behind-the-scenes processes and calculations using pivot tables.

Using VBA to Create Pivot Tables

First you need to know how to enable VBA in your Excel. If by default, VBA is disabled in your own copy of Excel/Office, then before you can start using VBA, you need to enable macros in the **Trust Center**.

Follow these steps:
1. Click the **File** menu to show the **Backstage View**.
2. In the left navigation, select **Options**. The **Excel Options** dialogue displays:
3. In the left navigation of Excel Options, select **Customize Ribbon**.
4. The right listbox has a list of main tabs available in Excel. By default, the checkbox for the Developer tab is unchecked. Select this tab to include it in the ribbon. Click **OK** to close **Excel Options**.

5. Click the **Developer** tab in the ribbon. As shown in Fig. 7.2, the Code group on the left side of the ribbon includes icons for the **Visual Basic Editor, Macros, Macro Recorder**, and **Macro Security**.

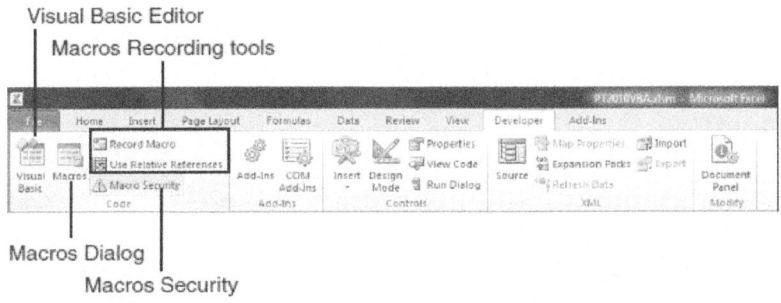

Fig. 7.2: VBA and Macro tools on the Excel Ribbon

6. Click the **Macro Security** icon. Excel opens the **Trust Center** where you have four security choices. These choices use different words from those used in Excel 97 through Excel 2003. Step 7 explains the choices.
7. Choose one of the following options:
    - **Disable all macros with notification**: This setting is equivalent to medium macro security in Excel 2003. When you open a workbook that contains macros, a message

appears alerting you that macros are in the workbook. If you expect macros to be in the workbook, you should click Options, Enable to allow the macros to run. This is the safest setting because it forces you to explicitly enable macros in each workbook.

- **Enable all macros**: This setting is not recommended because potentially dangerous code can run. However, this setting is equivalent to low macros security in Excel 2003. Because it can enable rogue macros to run in files that are sent to you by others, Microsoft recommends that you do not use this setting.

Visual Basic Editor

From Excel, press **Alt+F11** or select **Developer, Visual Basic** to open the **Visual Basic Editor**, as shown in Fig. 7.3. The three main sections of the VBA Editor are described here. If this is your first time using VBA, some of these items might be disabled. Follow the instructions given in the following list to make sure that each is enabled.

Fig. 7.3: The Visual Basic Editor (VBE)

Project Explorer: This pane displays a hierarchical tree of all open workbooks. Expand the tree to see the worksheets and code modules present in the workbook. If the Project Explorer is not visible, enable it by pressing **Ctrl+R**.

Properties window: The Properties window is important when you begin to program user forms. It has some use when you are writing normal code, so enable it by pressing **F4**.

Code window: This is the area where you write your code. Code is stored in one or more code modules attached to your workbook. To add a code module to a workbook, select **Insert**, **Module** from the **VBA** menu.

Visual Basic Tools

Visual Basic is a powerful development environment. Although this chapter cannot offer a complete course on VBA, if you are new to VBA, you should take advantage of these important tools:

As you begin to type code, Excel might offer a drop-down with valid choices. This feature, known as **AutoComplete**, enables you to type code faster and eliminate typing mistakes.

For assistance on any keyword, put the cursor in the keyword and press **F1**. You might need an installation DVDs because the VBA help file can be excluded from the installation of Office 2010/2013/2016.

Excel checks each line of code as you finish it. Lines in **error** appear in red. **Comments** appear in green. You can add a comment by typing a single apostrophe. Use lots of comments so you can remember what each section of code is doing.

Despite the aforementioned error checking, Excel might still encounter an error at runtime. If this happens, click the **Debug** button. The line that caused the error is highlighted in yellow. Hover your mouse cursor over any variable to see the current value of the variable.

When you are in Debug mode, use the Debug menu to step line by line through code. If you have a wide monitor, try arranging the **Excel window** and the **VBA window** side by side. This way, you can see the effect of running a line of code on the worksheet.

Other great debugging tools are **breakpoints**, the **Watch window**, the **Object Browser**, and the **Immediate** window. You should read about these tools in the Excel VBA Help menu.

Understanding Object-Oriented Code

VBA is an **object-oriented language**. Most lines of VBA code follow the **Noun.Verb** syntax. However, in VBA, it is called **Object.Method**. Examples of objects are **workbooks, worksheets, cells**, or **ranges of cells**. Methods can be typical Excel actions, such as **.Copy, .Paste**, and **.PasteSpecial**.

Many methods allow adverbs—parameters you use to specify how to perform the method. If you see a construct with **a :=** (colon and equal signs), you know that the macro recorder is describing how the method should work.

You also might see the type of code in which you assign a value to the adjectives of an object. In VBA, adjectives are called **properties**. If you set **ActiveCell.Font.ColorIndex = 3**, you are setting the font color of the active cell to red. Note that when you are dealing with properties, there is only an = (equal sign), not a := (colon and equal signs).

You need to master a few simple techniques to write efficient VBA code. These techniques help you make the jump to writing effective code.

Writing Code to Handle Any Size Data Range

The macro recorder hard-codes the fact that your data is in a range, such as **A1:L87601**. Although this hard-coding works for today's data set, it might not work as you get new data sets. You need to write code that can deal with different size data sets.

The macro recorder uses syntax such as **Range("H12")** to refer to a cell. However, it is more flexible to use **Cells(12, 8)** to refer to the cell in **Row 12, Column 8**. Similarly, the macro recorder refers to a rectangular range as **Range("A1:L87601")**. However, it is more flexible to use the **Cells** syntax to refer to the upper-left corner of the range, and then use the **Resize()** syntax to refer to the number of rows and columns in the range. The equivalent way to describe the preceding range is **Cells(1, 1).Resize(87601,12)**. This approach is more flexible because you can replace any of the numbers with a variable.

In the Excel user interface, you can use the **End** key on the keyboard to jump to the end of a range of data. If you move the cell pointer to the final row on the worksheet and press the End key followed by the **up-arrow** key, the cell pointer jumps to the last row with data. The equivalent of doing this in VBA is to use the following code:

Range("A1048576").End(xlUp).Select

You do not need to select this cell; you just need to find the row number that contains the last row. The following code locates this row and saves the row number to a variable named **FinalRow**:

FinalRow = Range("A1048576").End(xlUp).Row

There is nothing magic about the variable name **FinalRow**. You could call this variable x, y, or even your dog's name. However, because VBA enables you to use meaningful variable names, you should use something such as FinalRow to describe the final row.

You also can find the final column in a data set. If you are relatively sure that the data set begins in Row 1, you can use the **End** key in combination with the **left-arrow** key to jump from **Cell XFD1** to the last column with data. To generalize for the possibility that the code is running in legacy versions of Excel, you can use the following code:

FinalCol = Cells(1, Columns.Count).End(xlToLeft).Column

Using Super-Variables: Object Variables

In typical programming languages, a variable holds a single value. You might use x = 4 to assign a value of 4 to the variable x.

Think about a single cell in Excel. Many properties describe a cell. A cell might contain a value such as 4, but the cell also has a font size, a font color, a row, a column, possibly a formula, possibly a comment, a list of precedents, and more. It is possible in VBA to create a super-variable that contains all the information about a cell or about any object. A statement to create a typical variable such as **x = Range("A1")** assigns the current value of A1 to the variable x.

However, you can use the Set keyword to create an object variable:

Set x = Range("A1")

You have now created a super-variable that contains all the properties of the cell. Instead of having a variable with only one value, you have a variable in which you can access the value of many properties associated with that variable. You can reference x.Formula to learn the formula in A1 or x.Font.ColorIndex to learn the color of the cell.

Important Tip: The examples in this chapter frequently set up an object variable called **PT** to refer to the entire pivot table. This way, any time that the code would generally refer to **ActiveSheet.PivotTables**("PivotTable1"), you can specify **PT** to avoid typing the longer text.

Using With and End With to Shorten Code

You will frequently find that you are making several changes to the pivot table. Although the following code is explained later in this chapter, all these lines of code are changing settings in the pivot table:

PT.NullString = 0
PT.RepeatAllLabels xlRepeatLabels
PT.ColumnGrand = False
PT.RowGrand = False
PT.RowAxisLayout xlTabularRow
PT.TableStyle2 = "PivotStyleMedium10"
PT.TableStyleRowStripes = True

For all those lines of code, the VBA engine has to figure out what you mean by **PT**. Your code executes faster if you only refer to PT once. Add an initial line of **With PT**. Then, all the remaining lines do not need to start with PT. Any line that starts with a period is assumed to be referring to the object in the With statement. Finish the code block using an End With statement:

```
With PT
.NullString = 0
.RepeatAllLabels xlRepeatLabels
.ColumnGrand = False
.RowGrand = False
.RowAxisLayout xlTabularRow
.TableStyle2 = "PivotStyleMedium10"
.TableStyleRowStripes = True
End With
```

Building a Pivot Table in Excel VBA

Practice Project 3

This project does not mean to imply that you use VBA to build pivot tables to give to your clients. Instead, the purpose of this project is to give you strong foundation in VBA programming, and to remind you that pivot tables can be used as a means to an end. You can use a pivot table to extract a summary of data and then use that summary elsewhere. So open a new workbook in your VBE and start coding with me!

In **Excel 2000 and newer**, you first build a pivot cache object to describe the input area of the data:

```
Dim WSD As Worksheet
Dim PTCache As PivotCache
Dim PT As PivotTable
Dim PRange As Range
Dim FinalRow As Long
Dim FinalCol As Long
Set WSD = Worksheets("Data")

' Delete any prior pivot tables
For Each PT In WSD.PivotTables
PT.TableRange2.Clear
Next PT
' Define input area and set up a Pivot Cache
```

```
FinalRow = WSD.Cells(Rows.Count, 1).End(xlUp).Row
    FinalCol = WSD.Cells(1, Columns.Count).End(xlToLeft).Column
    Set PRange = WSD.Cells(1, 1).Resize(FinalRow, FinalCol)
    Set PTCache = ActiveWorkbook.PivotCaches.Add(SourceType:=xlDatabase, _
        SourceData:=PRange)
```

After defining the pivot cache, use the CreatePivotTable method to create a blank pivot table based on the defined pivot cache:

```
Set PT = PTCache.CreatePivotTable(TableDestination:=
    WSD.Cells(2, FinalCol + 2).TableName:="PivotTable1")
```

In the **Create PivotTable** method, you specify the output location and optionally give the table a name. After running this line of code, you have a strange-looking blank pivot table, like the one shown in Fig. 7.4 You now have to use code to drop fields onto the table.

Fig. 7.4: Immediately after you use the Create PivotTable method, Excel gives you a blank pivot table that is not useful.

If you choose the Defer Layout Update setting in the user interface to build the pivot table, Excel does not recalculate the pivot table after you drop each field onto the table. By default in VBA, Excel calculates the pivot table as you execute each step of building the table. This could require the pivot table to be executed a half-dozen times before you get to the final result.

To speed up your code execution, you can temporarily turn off calculation of the pivot table by using the ManualUpdate property:

```
PT.ManualUpdate = True
```

You can now run through the steps needed to lay out the pivot table. In the **.AddFields** method, you can specify one or more fields that should be in the row, column, or filter area of the pivot table.

The **RowFields** parameter enables you to define fields that appear in the Row Labels layout area of the PivotTable Field List. The **ColumnFields** parameter corresponds to the Column Labels layout area. The **PageFields** parameter corresponds to the Report Filter layout area.

The following line of code populates a pivot table with two fields in the row area and one field in the column area:

```
' Set up the row & column fields
PT.AddFields RowFields:=Array("Category", "Product"), _
ColumnFields:="Region"
```

Important Tip: If you are adding a single field to an area such as Region to the Column area, you only need to specify the name of the field in quotes. If you are adding two or more fields, you have to include that list inside the array function.

Although the row, column, and page fields of the pivot table can be handled with the **.AddFields** method, it is best to add fields to the Data area using the code described in the next section.

Adding Fields to the Data Area

When you are adding fields to the Data area of the pivot table, there are many settings that you would rather control rather than let Excel's intellisense decide.

Say that you are building a report with revenue. You likely want to sum the revenue. If you do not explicitly specify the calculation, Excel scans through the data in the underlying data. If 100 percent of the revenue columns are numeric, Excel sums. If one cell is blank or contains text, Excel decides to count the revenue. This produces confusing results.

Because of this possible variability, you should never use the DataFields argument in the AddFields method. Instead, change the property of the field to xlDataField. You can then specify the Function to be xlSum.

While you are setting up the data field, you can change several other properties within the same With...End With block.

The Position property is useful when adding multiple fields to the data area. Specify 1 for the first field, 2 for the second field, and so on.

By default, Excel renames a Revenue field to have a strange name like Sum of Revenue. You can use the .Name property to change that heading back to something normal. Note that you cannot reuse the word Revenue as a name, but you can use "Revenue " (with a space).

You are not required to specify a number format, but it can make the resulting pivot table easier to understand and only takes an extra line of code:

```
' Set up the data fields
With PT.PivotFields("Revenue")
.Orientation = xlDataField
.Function = xlSum
.Position = 1
.NumberFormat = "#,##0"
.Name = "Revenue "
End With
```

Formatting the Pivot Table

Microsoft introduced the Compact Layout for pivot tables in Excel 2007. There are 3 layouts available in Excel 2010, 2013 and 2016. Excel should default to using the Tabular layout. This is good because tabular view is the one that makes the most sense. It cannot hurt to add one line of code to ensure that you get the desired layout:

```
PT.RowAxisLayout xlTabularRow
```

In tabular layout, each field in the row area is in a different column. Subtotals always appear at the bottom of each group. This is the layout that has been around the longest and is most conducive to reusing the pivot table report for further analysis.

The Excel user interface frequently defaults to Compact layout. In this layout, multiple columns fields are stacked up into a single column on the left side of the pivot table. To create this layout, use the following code:

PT.RowAxisLayout xlCompactRow

The one limitation of tabular layout is that you cannot show the totals at the top of each group. If you would need to do this, you want to switch to the Outline layout and show totals at the top of the group:

PT.RowAxisLayout xlOutlineRow
PT.SubtotalLocation xlAtTop

Your pivot table inherits the table style settings selected as the default on whatever computer happens to run the code. If you would like control over the final format, you can explicitly choose a table style. The following code applies banded rows and a medium table style:

' Format the pivot table
PT.ShowTableStyleRowStripes = True
PT.TableStyle2 = "PivotStyleMedium10"

At this point, you have given VBA all the settings required to correctly generate the pivot table. If you set ManualUpdate to False , Excel calculates and draws the pivot table. Thereafter, you can immediately set this back to True by using this code:

' Calc the pivot table
PT.ManualUpdate = False
PT.ManualUpdate = True

At this point, you have a complete pivot table like the one shown in Fig. 7.5:

Sum of Revenue		Region	
Category	Product	Midwest	North
⊟ Bar Equipment	Bar Cover	1,328	
	Cocktail Shaker 28 Oz	4,607	1,681
	Commercial Bar Blender	1,704	
	Garnish Center	455	51
	Glass Rimmers Triple Brushes	8,760	3,360
	Glass Rimmers Twin Brushes	1,278	846
	High Power Blender Easy-To-Clean El	1,500	
	High Power Blender With Paddle Switc	1,125	
	One Gallon Blender	16,540	5,440
	Speed Rail 10 Quart/Liter Bottle Capac	753	369
	Speed Rail 5 Quart/Liter Bottle Capacit	989	184
	Speed Rail 8 Quart/Liter Bottle Capacity		
	Spindle Drink Mixer Single Spindle $ 2	1,650	
	Spindle Drink Mixers 32 Oz. S/S Contai	1,428	83
	Spindle Drink Mixers 48 Oz. Poly. Conta	21,505	8,131
Bar Equipment Total		63,621	20,145
⊟ Commercial Appliance	2 1/2 Qt. Cap. Batch Bowl	3,520	4,154
	2 1/2 Qt. Cap. Batch Bowl/Continuous Fe	7,750	4,340
	2 1/2 Qt. Cap. Dicing Food Processor	30,689	
	4 Qt. Cap. Batch Bow	36,998	3,436

Fig. 7.5: Fewer than 50 lines of code create this pivot table in less than a second

Below is the complete code used to generate the pivot table:

```
Dim PRange As Range
Dim FinalRow As Long
Set WSD = Worksheets("Data")
' Delete any prior pivot tables
For Each PT In WSD.PivotTables
PT.TableRange2.Clear
Next PT
WSD.Range("N1:AZ1").EntireColumn.Clear
' Define input area and set up a Pivot Cache
FinalRow = WSD.Cells(Application.Rows.Count, 1).End(xlUp).Row
FinalCol = WSD.Cells(1, Application.Columns.Count). _
End(xlToLeft).Column
Set PRange = WSD.Cells(1, 1).Resize(FinalRow, FinalCol)
Set PTCache = ActiveWorkbook.PivotCaches.Add(SourceType:= _
xlDatabase, SourceData:=PRange.Address)
' Create the Pivot Table from the Pivot Cache
Set PT = PTCache.CreatePivotTable(TableDestination:=WSD. _
Cells(2, FinalCol + 2), TableName:="PivotTable1")
' Turn off updating while building the table
PT.ManualUpdate = True
' Set up the row & column fields
PT.AddFields RowFields:=Array("Category", "Product"), _
ColumnFields:="Region"
' Set up the data fields
With PT.PivotFields("Revenue")
.Orientation = xlDataField
```

```
.Function = xlSum
.Position = 1
.NumberFormat = "#,##0"
End With
' Format the pivot table
PT.RowAxisLayout xlTabularRow
PT.ShowTableStyleRowStripes = True
PT.TableStyle2 = "PivotStyleMedium10"
' Calc the pivot table
PT.ManualUpdate = False
PT.ManualUpdate = True
WSD.Activate
Cells(2, FinalCol + 2).Select
End Sub
```

Chapter 8: Advanced Tips, Tricks & Techniques

To bring this book to a sweet end, I want to give you some useful advanced tips, tricks and techniques that will make you work faster, save your time when working on Pivot tables and other Excel functions.

1. Force Pivot Tables to Refresh Automatically.
In some situations, you might need to have your pivot tables refresh themselves automatically. For instance, suppose you created a pivot table report for your manager. You might not be able to trust that he will refresh the pivot table when needed.

You can force each pivot table to automatically refresh when the workbook opens by following these steps:

1. Right-click your pivot table and select **PivotTable Options**.
2. In the activated dialog box, select the **Data** tab.
3. Select the **Refresh Data** When Opening the File property check box.

When this property is activated, the pivot table refreshes itself each time the workbook in which it's located is opened.

2. Refresh All Pivot Tables in a Workbook at the Same Time.
When you have multiple pivot tables in a workbook, refreshing all of them can be bothersome. There are several ways to avoid the hassle of manually refreshing multiple pivot tables. Here are a couple options:

Option 1: You can configure each pivot table in your workbook to automatically refresh when the workbook opens. To do so, right-click your pivot table and select **PivotTable Options**. This activates the PivotTable Options dialog box. Then, select the Data tab and select the Refresh Data When Opening the File property check box. After you have configured all pivot tables in the workbook, they automatically refresh when the workbook is opened.

Option 2: You can create a macro to refresh each pivot table in the workbook. This option is ideal when you need to refresh your pivot tables on demand, rather than only when the workbook opens. The idea is to start recording a macro. While the macro is recording, simply go to each pivot table in your workbook and refresh. After all pivot tables are refreshed, stop recording. The result is a macro that can be fired any time you need to refresh all pivot tables.

Option 3: You can use VBA to refresh all pivot tables in the workbook on demand. This option can be used when it is impractical to record and maintain macros that refresh all pivot tables. This approach entails the use of the RefreshAll method of the Workbook object. To employ this technique, start a new module and enter the following code:

```
Sub Refresh_All()
ThisWorkbook.RefreshAll
End Sub
```

You can now call this procedure any time you want to refresh all pivot tables within your workbook.

3: Sort Data Items in a Unique Order (Not Ascending or Descending)

Fig. 8.0 shows the default sequence of regions in a pivot table report. Alphabetically, the regions are shown in sequence of Midwest, North, South, and West. If your company is based in California, company traditions might dictate that the West region should be shown first, followed by Midwest, North, and South. Unfortunately, neither an ascending sort order nor a descending sort order can help you.

	A	B	C	D	E	F
1						
2						
3	Sum of Sales_Amount	Column Labels				
4	Row Labels	MIDWEST	NORTH	SOUTH	WEST	Grand Total
5	Cleaning & Housekeeping Services	$174,518	$534,282	$283,170	$146,623	$1,138,593
6	Facility Maintenance and Repair	$463,077	$606,747	$846,515	$444,820	$2,361,158
7	Fleet Maintenance	$448,800	$610,791	$1,046,231	$521,976	$2,627,798
8	Green Plants and Foliage Care	$93,562	$155,021	$157,821	$870,379	$1,276,783
9	Landscaping/Grounds Care	$190,003	$299,309	$335,676	$365,928	$1,190,915
10	Predictive Maintenance/Preventative Maintenance	$478,928	$572,860	$472,045	$655,092	$2,178,925
11	Grand Total	$1,848,887	$2,779,009	$3,141,458	$3,004,818	$10,774,172
12						
13						

Fig. 8.0: Default sequence of regions in a pivot table report

You can rearrange data items in your pivot table manually by simply typing the exact name of the data item where you would like to see its data. You can also drag the data item where you want it. To solve the problem in this example, you simply type the word **West** in cell **B4**, and then press Enter. The pivot table responds by resequencing the regions. The $3 million in sales for the West region automatically moves from column E to column B. The remaining regions move over to the next two columns.

4: Turn Pivot Tables into Hard Data

You created your pivot table only to summarize and shape your data. You do not want to keep the source data or the pivot table with all its overhead.

Turning your pivot table into hard data enables you to utilize the results of the pivot table without having to deal with the source data or a pivot cache. How you turn your pivot table into hard data depends on how much of your pivot table you are going to copy.

If you are copying just a portion of your pivot table, do the following steps:

1. Select the data you want to copy from the pivot table, and then right-click and select **Copy**.
2. Right-click anywhere on a spreadsheet and select **Paste**.

If you are copying your entire pivot table, follow these steps:

1. Select the entire pivot table, right-click, and select Copy.
2. Right-click anywhere on a spreadsheet and select **Paste Special**.
3. Select Values, and then click **OK**.

Important Tip: You might want to consider removing any **subtotals** before turning your pivot table into hard data. Subtotals typically aren't very useful when you are creating a **standalone** data set.

To remove the subtotals from your pivot table, first identify the field for which subtotals are being calculated. Then, right-click the field's header (either in the pivot table itself or in the **PivotTable Field List**) and select **Field Settings**. Selecting this option opens the Field Settings dialog box. Here, you change the Subtotals option to **None**. After you click **OK**, your subtotals are removed.

5: Fill the Empty Cells Left by Row Fields
When you turn a pivot table into hard data, you are left not only with the values created by the pivot table, but also the pivot table's data structure. For example, the data in Fig. 8.1 came from a pivot table that had a tabular layout.

Notice that the Market field kept the same row structure it had when this data was in the row area of the pivot table. It would be unwise to use this table anywhere else without filling in the empty cells left by the row field, but how do you easily fill these empty cells?

	A	B	C	D
3	Region	Market	Product_Description	Sum of Sales_Amount
4	⊟ MIDWEST	⊟ DENVER	Cleaning & Housekeeping Services	$12,564
5			Facility Maintenance and Repair	$160,324
6			Fleet Maintenance	$170,190
7			Green Plants and Foliage Care	$42,409
8			Landscaping/Grounds Care	$73,622
9			Predictive Maintenance/Preventative Maintenance	$186,475
10		DENVER Total		$645,583
11		⊟ KANSASCITY	Cleaning & Housekeeping Services	$65,439
12			Facility Maintenance and Repair	$132,120
13			Fleet Maintenance	$133,170
14			Green Plants and Foliage Care	$35,315
15			Landscaping/Grounds Care	$52,442
16			Predictive Maintenance/Preventative Maintenance	$156,412
17		KANSASCITY Total		$574,899
18		⊟ TULSA	Cleaning & Housekeeping Services	$96,515
19			Facility Maintenance and Repair	$170,632
20			Fleet Maintenance	$145,440
21			Green Plants and Foliage Care	$15,838
22			Landscaping/Grounds Care	$63,939
23			Predictive Maintenance/Preventative Maintenance	$136,041
24		TULSA Total		$628,405
25	MIDWEST Total			$1,848,887

Fig. 8.1: It would be impractical to use this data anywhere else without filling in the empty cells left by the row field

Excel 2010, 2013 and 2016 actually provides you very effective ways of fixing this problem. One of them is explained below:

Implement the New Repeat All Data Items Feature
You can apply Excel's new **Repeat Item Labels** functionality. This new feature ensures that all item labels are repeated to create a solid block of contiguous cells. To implement this feature, place your cursor anywhere in your pivot table. Then, go up to the Ribbon and select Design, Report Layout, **Repeat All Item** labels (see Fig. 8.2).

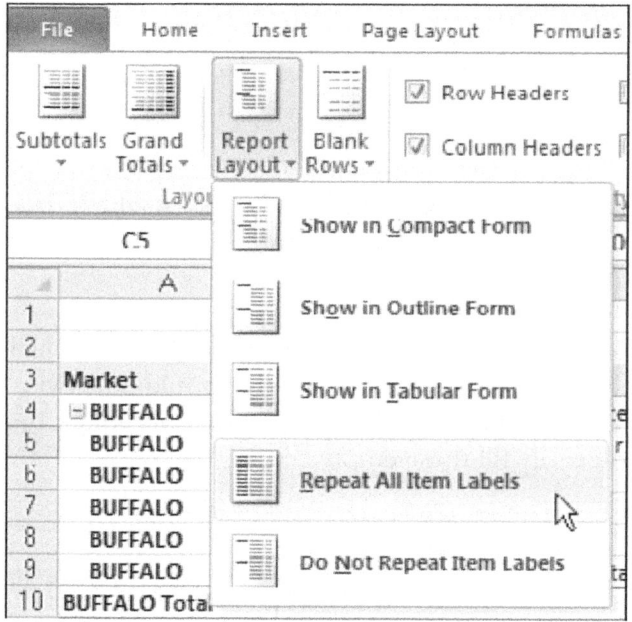

Fig. 8.2: The Repeat All Item Labels option enables you to show your pivot data in one contiguous block of data

Fig. 8.3 shows what a pivot table with this feature applied looks like:

	A	B	C	D
1				
2				
3	Region	Market	Product_Description	Sum of Sales_Amount
4	⊟MIDWEST	⊟DENVER	Cleaning & Housekeeping Services	$12,564
5	MIDWEST	DENVER	Facility Maintenance and Repair	$160,324
6	MIDWEST	DENVER	Fleet Maintenance	$170,190
7	MIDWEST	DENVER	Green Plants and Foliage Care	$42,409
8	MIDWEST	DENVER	Landscaping/Grounds Care	$73,622
9	MIDWEST	DENVER	Predictive Maintenance/Preventative Maintenance	$186,475
10	MIDWEST	DENVER Total		$645,583
11	MIDWEST	⊟KANSASCITY	Cleaning & Housekeeping Services	$65,439
12	MIDWEST	KANSASCITY	Facility Maintenance and Repair	$132,120
13	MIDWEST	KANSASCITY	Fleet Maintenance	$133,170
14	MIDWEST	KANSASCITY	Green Plants and Foliage Care	$35,315
15	MIDWEST	KANSASCITY	Landscaping/Grounds Care	$52,442
16	MIDWEST	KANSASCITY	Predictive Maintenance/Preventative Maintenance	$156,412
17	MIDWEST	KANSASCITY Total		$574,899
18	MIDWEST	⊟TULSA	Cleaning & Housekeeping Services	$96,515
19	MIDWEST	TULSA	Facility Maintenance and Repair	$170,632
20	MIDWEST	TULSA	Fleet Maintenance	$145,440
21	MIDWEST	TULSA	Green Plants and Foliage Care	$15,838
22	MIDWEST	TULSA	Landscaping/Grounds Care	$63,939
23	MIDWEST	TULSA	Predictive Maintenance/Preventative Maintenance	$136,041
24	MIDWEST	TULSA Total		$628,405
25	MIDWEST Total			$1,848,887

Fig. 8.3: The Repeat All Item Labels option fills all cells with data items

Conclusion

Dear reader, I hope that you have found the information in this book useful. You may find some of the concepts we have covered in this book confusing at first. However, with time and effort, you will be able to achieve many great things with Excel's Pivot tables and charts, and create anything you want.

I wish you the best of luck in your endeavors. Send me an email if you need further help or if you have questions.

Regards,
A. J. Wright
Email:gregorywillis70@gmail.com

Made in the USA
Las Vegas, NV
17 January 2021